T0195600

# Math Problem Solving Strategies

# NO PROBLEM!

## Taking the Problem Out of Mathematical Problem Solving

Written by **Joan Vydra** and **Jean McCall**
Illustrated by **Dean Crawford Jr.**

First published 2005 by Prufrock Press Inc.

Published 2021 by Routledge
605 Third Avenue, New York, NY 10017
2 Park Square, Milton Park, Abingdon, Oxon OX14 4RN

*Routledge is an imprint of the Taylor & Francis Group, an informa business*

© 2005 by Taylor & Francis

All rights reserved. No part of this book may be reprinted or reproduced or utilised in any form or by any electronic, mechanical, or other means, now known or hereafter invented, including photocopying and recording, or in any information storage or retrieval system, without permission in writing from the publishers.

Notice:
Product or corporate names may be trademarks or registered trademarks and are used only for identification and explanation without intent to infringe.

ISBN 13: 978-1-59363-112-3 (pbk)

Edited by Dianne Draze

Routledge
Taylor & Francis Group
NEW YORK AND LONDON

# Contents

# Introduction

What is mathematics? It is more than numbers, more than operations, more than shapes, and more than statistics. Mathematics is a way of thinking and reasoning. This type of thinking is used to solve problems in all areas of our world. It allows us not only to compute, but also to measure, predict, draw, navigate, and form relationships. The role of a mathematician does not involve adding columns of numbers. It involves using logic, looking for patterns, discovering rules, and organizing data. It does involve the use of computational skills, but more importantly, it calls for the use of imagination, reasoning, and flexibility. It is this type of thinking that will be developed by the exercises in this book.

There are eight problem solving strategies that are presented in this text. They are:

- guess and check
- make a table
- make an organized list
- look for a pattern
- act out or use manipulatives
- use logic
- simplify or work backwards
- make a diagram or drawing

While there are other problem-solving strategies that mathematicians use, these are the strategies that will allow elementary-age students to solve mathematical problems most consistently.

This program of daily problem solving is designed for use in either regular or gifted classrooms as a supplement to the prescribed math text. The first eight weeks of this program are devoted to learning one new strategy per week, practicing the strategy by solving one problem per day. The rest of the year, a variety of problems are provided that will allow students opportunities to apply these strategies.

There are several steps that students will go through as they attempt to solve each problem. These are:

- reading the problem
- finding the important information
- analyzing the problem and selecting strategies
- finding the solution
- checking and verifying the solution

These are not formal steps that students should be forced to go through, but rather guides that you may wish to remind students about from time to time. In general, before students attempt to select a problem-solving strategy, they should carefully read the problem, decide what the problem is asking, and sort out the important information. When students are finished with their calculations, it is important to encourage them to look at their answers, check their calculations, and ask, "does it make sense?"

Problems can be presented by being written on the board, duplicated, or projected with an overhead projector. Students should be encouraged to keep a problem solving notebook to use on a daily basis throughout the year. They will probably find that work done early in the year will be a helpful reference as the problems get more difficult.

The problems to be presented during the first eight weeks of this program are given with teaching suggestions and complete answers. It is important that each strategy be thoroughly taught during these first eight weeks. For many students, it will be a first exposure to problems that need thinking strategies and not just computational expertise. Problems presented during the remainder of the school year may be solved by individual students or used in small cooperative learning teams. If working in a cooperative group, students will have to decide the appropriate strategy and then agree on the correct answer.

Whether working alone or in a group, it is worthwhile to have students discuss the problems after they have completed them. Don't just give the correct answer; invite students to talk about their thinking and talk about the strategies that were involved. In this program, the process is often more important than the end product, and discussion allows students to compare the various processes.

Use of calculators are a teaching option, although certainly not a necessity for intermediate children. The emphasis should be on the problem solving and not necessarily on the computational skills involved. To this end, if calculators remove computational frustrations and allow for freer thought, make them available for student use whenever possible.

The role of the instructor in this program is to facilitate problem solving by creating a climate that is conducive to experimentation and exploration. This means giving students adequate time for problem solving and also encouraging them to think about several possible strategies for solving problems. It means modeling problem-solving behaviors and also allowing time for students to discuss their thinking.

## Problem 1

Mr. K. Nine has two dogs named Barnum and Bailey. He has 25 dog biscuits to split between the two dogs so that Barnum will get exactly 11 more than Bailey. How many biscuits will each dog get?

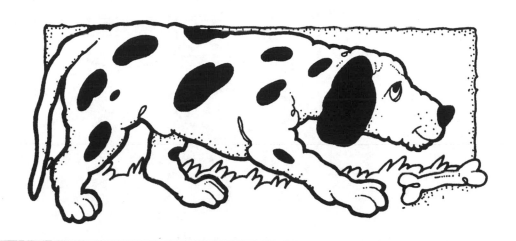

## Problem 2

I. M. Greedy has 7 coins that have a total value of 48¢. What coins does Mr. Greedy have?

Number of quarters ___

Number of dimes ___

Number of nickels ___

Number of pennies ___

7

© Prufrock Press Inc • No Problem!

## Problem 3

Mazie Muddler has the following diagram and has to put five different numbers (none larger than 8) in each oval so that the sums of both diagonals are 15.

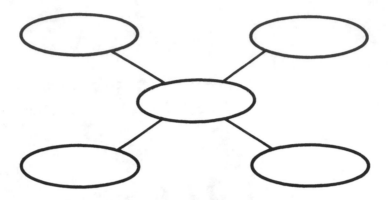

## Problem 4

It costs 15¢ to mail a postcard and 25¢ for a letter. Miss Handle wrote to thirteen friends and spent $2.65 for postage. How many letters and postcards did she send?

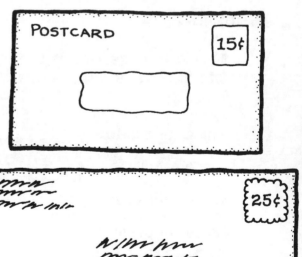

© Prufrock Press Inc • No Problem!

## Problem 5

Cara Mell has 56 cookies in her cupboard. She has eighteen more chocolate cookies than gingersnaps. If there are only two types of cookies, how many of each kind are there?

## Bonus Problem

April Day, Peter Rabbit, and Marsha Mallow all joined the Annual Easter Egg Hunt at the local park. When the hunt was over, the three friends sat down together and counted their eggs. April and Peter had a combined total of 25 eggs. Peter and Marsha had a combined total of 23 eggs. April and Marsha had a combined total of 24 eggs. How many eggs did each child find?

9

© Prufrock Press Inc • No Problem!

The guess and check strategy is used when there are several possible combinations of answers, only one of which is correct. Students using this strategy guess an answer, check to see if it is correct, and continue eliminating possibilities as they get closer to the solution that fits the given clues.

## Problem 1

In the guess and check strategy, students start with a reasonable guess and then work from that answer. For this problem, students need to start with either Barnum or Bailey's biscuits. For instance, if a student predicts that Bailey has 6 dog biscuits, then Barnum must have 11 more, or 17. The sum of 23 is short the needed number of 25, so students will need to make an adjusted guess based on this first result.

Some students might want to start a table of all the combinations of numbers that total 25, but this is not as desirable as the guess and check strategy because of the extra steps involved.

**Answer**: Barnum will get 18 dog biscuits and Bailey will get 7 dog biscuits.

## Problem 2

Students are going to make a guess about the coins I. M. has, calculate the results, and then proceed from that point. Guess and check is based on logical assumptions, and always starts from the knowns. In this particular problem, students should immediately figure out that at least three of the coins are pennies — this is the known starting point. It will be helpful for students to make a chart, similar to the one shown below.

| quarters | dimes | nickels | pennies | Total |
|----------|-------|---------|---------|-------|
| 1 | 0 | 3 | 3 | 43¢ |
| 1 | 3 | 0 | 3 | 58¢ |

**Answer**: The seven coins are 1 quarter, 1 dime, 2 nickels, and 3 pennies.

## Problem 3

In this, as in other guess and check problems, students need to start with a reasonable guess and then work from that point. One way that many students start is to list some of the possibilities of three numbers less than 8 totalling 15. Other students start by putting numbers in the five ovals and checking the results. Either methodology is acceptable, although you might feel more comfortable going through the former with the students. This will depend, at least in part, on their success on the previous two days.

A way to further limit or qualify the problem is to write the problem on the board as follows: *Mazie Muddler has the following diagram and has to find five different numbers with a sum of 26 and put one number in each oval so that the sums of both diagonals are 15.* In this case the only correct answer is 8-4-3 and 6-4-5.

**Problem 3**, continued
**Answer:**
  One row might read: 8 – 4 – 3 and the other 6 – 4 – 5
  One row might read: 8 – 3 – 4 and the other 7 – 3 – 5
  One row might read: 8 – 2 – 5 and the other 7 – 2 – 6
  One row might read: 8 – 1 – 6 and the other 9 – 1 – 5
  One row might read: 8 – 5 – 2 and the other 7 – 5 – 3
  One row might read: 8 – 6 – 1 and the other 7 – 6 – 2

## Problem 4

Once again, students are going to start with a reasonable guess, compare it to the given answer of $2.65 and then see if the next guess needs to be higher or lower. What makes this easier is that students are given a framework — they are told that the total number sent is thirteen. A chart similar to the one given below might facilitate understanding and prevent replication of effort.

| postcards | letters | total postage |
|-----------|---------|---------------|
| 10 | 3 | $2.25 |
| 5 | 8 | $2.75 |

**Answer:** Miss Handle sent 6 postcards and 7 letters.

## Problem 5

This problem is similar to the first one, the problem about the dog biscuits. At this point in time, it is suggested that you give students the problem on the board with **no instruction**. This will allow you to ascertain whether or not the students have learned the guess and check strategy.

**Answer:** Cara Mell has 37 chocolate cookies and 19 gingersnaps.

## Bonus Problem

In this problem, students are presented with several variables. It is best if they begin with one of the combinations, for instance the fact that April and Peter together have 25 eggs. They can then begin making guesses about how many each person might have and check these numbers against the other criteria (totals for April and Marsha and for Marsha and Peter).

**Answer:** April found 13 eggs
  Peter found 12 eggs
  Marsha found 11 eggs

© Prufrock Press Inc • *No Problem!*

## Problem 1

Claire Inett left a secret message for Vi Olin on one of the pages of their concert book. Vi knows that the number of the page the message is written on is less than 155 because this is the total number of pages in the book. Claire also told her that the page number is a 3-digit number, that one of the digits is 4, and that the total of all three digits in the number is 11. On what page is the message?

## Problem 2

Jill and Bill are two members of the Hill family. Jill is 8 years old and Bill is 9 years old. What will Bill's age be when the total of the digits in both their ages is once again 17?

© Prufrock Press Inc · No Problem!

## Problem 3

Percy Veer is training for the Olympic Marathon. When asked how many miles he runs each week, he is very evasive, but does give these clues:

- It is more than 150 miles.
- It is less than 225 miles.
- The number of miles is divisible by 5.
- The number of miles is divisible by 9.

## Problem 4

Artie Choke and Tom A. Toe both shop at the same local grocery store between five and six in the evening. The last time they saw each other was on Tuesday. Artie shops every five days and Tom shops every four days. What day of the week will they next run into each other at the store, assuming that the store is open seven days a week?

© Prufrock Press Inc • *No Problem!*

## Problem 5

Cookie Cutter is baking cookies. She has 100 cookies and will be putting three different kinds of decorations on the cookies. She lines up the cookies and puts frosting on every fifth cookie. Then she puts candies on every eighth cookie. Finally she gets out the cherries and puts one on every ninth cookie. How many of her cookies have all the decorations (frosting, candy, and a cherry)?

## Bonus Problem

Barb Wire adds 1 link to her paper chain every day. Chuck Stake adds 3 links to his chain every day. Barb's chain has 9 links right now, and Chuck's chain has 3 links right now. If they keep adding links at the same rate, how many days before Chuck's chain has exactly twice as many links as Barb's chain?

Using or making a table is a strategy useful in setting up an orderly arrangement of numbers (or other data). When the information is set up systematically, the solutions are more easily spotted.

## Problem 1

Students need to be taught to find the most logical place to start attacking the problem. In this case, Vi knows that the number is less than 155, but is a 3-digit number. She also knows that one of the digits is 4 and that the three digits will total 11. Students can start listing the 3-digit numbers that start with 1 and have 4 as either the second or third number. They can next check to see which of those numbers satisfies the final condition of totalling 11.

A table might start like this:

| 114 | 124 | 134 | 141 |
|-----|-----|-----|-----|
| no  | no  | no  | no  |

Answer: page 146

## Problem 2

The secret to solving this problem is carefully reading the problem and then constructing a table to show the ages and the sum of the digits in the two ages. The table should look like this:

| Jill | 8 | 9 | 10 | 11 | 12 | 13 | 14 | 15 | 16 | 17 |
|------|---|---|----|----|----|----|----|----|----|----|
| Bill | 9 | 10 | 11 | 12 | 13 | 14 | 15 | 16 | 17 | 18 |
| sum of digits | 17 | 10 | 3 | 5 | 7 | 9 | 11 | 13 | 15 | 17 |

**Answer**: Bill will be 18 and Jill will be 17 years old.

## Problem 3

Once again, this problem is simplified with a table. The only difficult part for students is finding a reasonable starting point. In this particular problem, it is logical to start with 155 (the next number after 150 divisible by 5) and then continue with the table until a number satisfies the other condition of being divisible by 9. Younger students might feel more comfortable with a calculator on this problem.

| 155 | 160 | 165 | 170 | 175 |
|-----|-----|-----|-----|-----|
| no  | no  | no  | no  | no  |

Answer: 180 miles

15                                                      © Prufrock Press Inc • *No Problem!*

## Problem 4

The type of chart needed for this problem is similar to the one needed for the Hill family age problem presented earlier. Students should figure out that the logical place to begin is the Tuesday of Tom's and Artie's last meeting. The chart that they will devise should look something like the following:

| Tues. | Wed. | Thurs. | Fri. | Sat. | Sun. | Mon. |
|-------|------|--------|------|------|------|------|
| A/T   |      |        |      | T    | A    |      |
|       | T    |        | A    |      | T    |      |
|       | A    |        | T    |      |      | A    |

**Answer**: The two men will next meet on a Monday.

## Problem 5

This problem will require a longer chart — a way for the children to calculate of all 100 cookies. One very easy way to do this is to take a piece of notebook paper and fold it in half lengthwise and then in half again, also lengthwise. Students need to count off 25 lines, mark the paper accordingly, and they now have the 100 spaces that they need to represent the cookies. The next step is to give each of the different decorations a code, such as an X for a candy, a circle for frosting, and a star for cherries. (These are only suggestions; students will have more fun working out their own symbols.) Students will then make the appropriate marks in the spaces that represent cookies and then check to see how many spaces have more than one mark on them.

An additional challenge in this problem would be to ask students to find how many cookies have no decorations on them, how many have one kind of decoration, and how many have two kinds of decorations and make a Venn diagram to represent these numbers.

**Answer**: Students will be surprised to find out that none of the cookies have all three decorations. Two cookies have both frosting and candies, two have both frosting and a cherry, and one has both a cherry and candies.

## Bonus Problem

In this problem, students will need to make a chart similar to the one below, showing the total number of links each person has each day.

| day   | 1 | 2  | 3  | 4  | 5  |
|-------|---|----|----|----|----|
| Barb  | 9 | 10 | 11 | 12 | 13 |
| Chuck | 3 | 6  | 9  | 12 | 15 |

**Answer**: It takes 15 days of adding links before Chuck has twice as many links as Barb. On the 16th day Chuck will have 48 links and Barb will have 24 links.

## Problem 1

List all of the three-digit numerals that can be made by using the numerals 4, 6, and 8 once in each numeral.

How many four-digit numerals can be made by using the numerals 2, 4, 6, and 8 once in each numeral?

## Problem 2

Katy Did has six pets of three different varieties — two dogs, two cats, and two lizards. Every time she goes out she takes three animals, one of each variety. She can take:

Polly or Petula Poodle
Tom or Ali Cat
Lizzie or Lily Lizard

How many combinations of animals are possible?

17

© Prufrock Press Inc • No Problem!

## Problem 3

Bob Bunglitt is practicing darts and decides to figure out how many different scores are possible if he uses exactly four darts and if all the darts hit in a numbered area. How many different scores are possible? What are these scores?

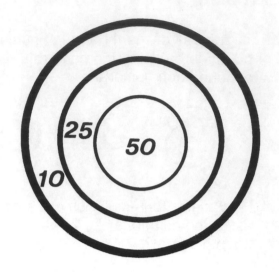

## Problem 4

Iva Fortune had 95¢. She spent 54¢. She received 41¢ change. How many different combinations of quarters, dimes, nickels, and pennies could she have received as change?

© Prufrock Press Inc · No Problem!

## Problem 5

In the Chinese Checker tournament, Mark Able, Anita Break, Jack Jumper, Ping Pong, and Chubby Checker all still need to play each other before the champion is announced. If each player plays all other remaining contestants, how many matches will be played altogether?

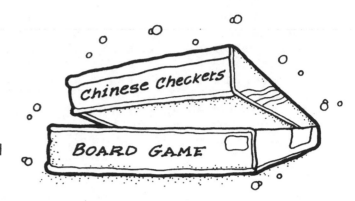

## Bonus Problem

Mary Meant loves the number eight. How many 8's will she write altogether if she writes the numbers 1 through 100?

© Prufrock Press Inc • *No Problem!*

Like the previous strategy of using a table, making an organized list helps sort data in a systematic way. This strategy is especially helpful when there are multiple data sources and too many things to remember.

Before introducing this technique, students need to be shown why organization is important. To do this, ask students to think of a number that is divisible by two and then randomly call on students to share their number. It usually takes only 8 or 9 responses before someone repeats an answer given earlier. It is then easy to make a case for approaching the problem in an organized fashion.

## Problem 1

To start the list of numerals with 4, 6, or 8, students need to remind themselves of the conditions of the problem. In this problem, the condition is that numbers can only be used once in each number. They can then proceed in a systematic fashion, making a list of all the numbers.

An added challenge is to give students the same three numbers, but this time remove any conditions concerning how many times a number may be used.

**Answer**: The 3-digit numerals are 468, 486, 648, 684, 864, and 846.
There are 24 different numerals that can be written using 2, 4, 6, and 8.

## Problem 2

Students will need to make a very systematic and orderly list of all possible combinations of three animals. A logical place to start is with Polly Poodle, listing all of the combinations possible with Polly.

A list might look something like the following:
Polly – Tom – Lizzie          Petula – Tom – Lizzie
Polly – Ali – Lizzie          Petula – Ali – Lizzie
Polly – Tom – Lily            Petula – Tom – Lily
Polly – Ali – Lily            Petula – Ali – Lily

**Answer**: 8 combinations

## Problem 3

Once again, a systematic list is the easiest way to make sure that all possibilities are noted. The list might start something like the following:

| 50 | 25 | 10 | Score |
|----|----|----|-------|
| 4  | 0  | 0  | 200   |
| 3  | 1  | 0  | 175   |
| 3  | 0  | 1  | 160   |

**Answer**: Fifteen different combinations with 15 unique scores are possible. The scores are 200, 175, 160, 150, 135, 125, 120, 110, 100, 95, 85, 80, 60, 55, and 40.

## Problem 4

This problem has multiple answers and might best be presented in list form. The list will be the most organized if done in fashion similar to the previous dart problem. The list might look something like the following:

| quarter | dime | nickel | penny | total |
|---------|------|--------|-------|-------|
| 1 | 1 | 1 | 1 | = 41¢ |

**Answer:**

If the first column is quarters, the second is dimes, the third is nickels, and the fourth is pennies, the 31 combinations are:

| | | | |
|---|---|---|---|
| 1 - 1 - 1 - 1 | 0 - 4 - 0 - 1 | 0 - 3 - 2 - 1 | 0 - 0 - 7 - 6 |
| 0 - 3 - 1 - 6 | 0 - 3 - 0 - 11 | 0 - 2 - 4 - 1 | 1 - 0 - 1 - 11 |
| 0 - 2 - 3 - 6 | 0 - 2 - 2 - 11 | 0 - 2 - 1 - 16 | 1 - 0 - 2 - 6 |
| 0 - 2 - 0 - 21 | 0 - 1 - 6 - 1 | 0 - 1 - 5 - 6 | 0 - 0 - 1 - 36 |
| 0 - 1 - 4 - 11 | 0 - 1 - 3 - 16 | 0 - 1 - 2 - 21 | 1 - 0 - 0 - 16 |
| 0 - 1 - 1 - 26 | 0 - 1 - 0 - 31 | 0 - 0 - 8 - 1 | 1 - 1 - 0 - 6 |
| 1 - 0 - 3 - 1 | 0 - 0 - 6 - 11 | 0 - 0 - 5 - 16 | 0 - 0 - 0 - 41 |
| 0 - 0 - 4 - 21 | 0 - 0 - 3 - 26 | 0 - 0 - 2 - 31 | |

## Problem 5

Once again, organizing the information is the most important part of solving this problem. Without the strategy of making a systematic list, most students will simply multiply five times five, the number of players. That strategy doesn't recognize the fact that if Mark plays Chubby, it is the same as Chubby playing Mark. Students will be able to solve this problem with either a chart or a list. It might look something like this:

| | |
|---|---|
| Mark vs. Anita | Mark vs. Jack |
| Mark vs. Ping | Mark vs. Chubby |
| Anita vs. Jack | Anita vs. Ping |
| Anita vs. Chubby | Jack vs. Ping |
| Jack vs. Chubby | Ping vs. Chubby |

**Answer:** (as above) 10 matches

## Bonus Problem

Students should attack this problem by making a list of all of the numbers that have 8 in the ones or ten's place and then count the number of 8's that appear. Since this problem asks for the number of 8's that will be written and not just the total number of numerals that have an 8 in them, students must count both 8's in the numeral 88.

**Answer:** She will write twenty (20) 8's.

© Prufrock Press Inc • *No Problem!*

## Problem 1

Bertha Busybee wants to label the hexagonal cells in the honeycomb using the letters A, B, C, D, E, and F in a systematic fashion. She started lettering the cells following a special pattern. Can you discover the pattern and fill in the letters for the blank cells?

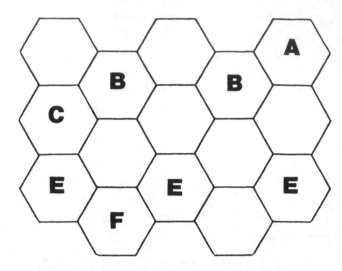

## Problem 2

Pat Tern decided to stump Ima Puzzle with the following sequences of names. Determine the pattern and supply a name on each line that will continue the pattern.

A. Al, Ben, Chad, _____

B. Jan, Kate, Libby, _____

C. Matilda, Lionel, Karen, _____

## Problem 3

The ladybug convention met in Tiger Lily's garden. On the first day there were 7 ladybugs. On the second day there were 15 ladybugs, and then 24 on the third day. At this rate, how many ladybugs will there be on the 8th day?

## Problem 4

Shelly Counter is researching sea shells and has discovered that the structure of a nautilus shell duplicates a numerical pattern discovered by the mathematician Fibonacci. The progression is:

1, 1, 2, 3, 5, 8, 13 . . .

What two numbers should come next in this series? ____ ____

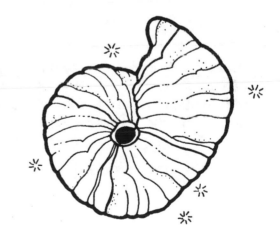

23

© Prufrock Press Inc • *No Problem!*

## Problem 5

Dee Sparing is having a difficult time learning patterns. Before she gets totally frustrated, help her by determining the patterns given below and then filling in the next two numbers for each given sequence.

A. 1, 4, 2, 5, 3, 6, 4, ___ , ___

B. 11, 30, 22, 40, 33, ___ , ___

C. 3, 6, 4, 8, 6, 12, ___ , ___

D. 5, 3, 8, 6, 11, 9, 14, ___ , ___

## Bonus Problem

Butch R. Block was trying to figure out the following patterns. Help Butch by supplying the next 2 numbers or letters for each sequence and describing the pattern for each sequence.

a. 1, 4, 9, 16, ___ , ___

b. B, C, E, F, H, I, ___ , ___

c. 100, 52, 28, 16, ___ , ___

d. Z, 1, W, 3, T, 5, ___ , ___

e. 1, 5, 10, 14, 28, ___ , ___

f. .5, .8, .6, .9, .7, ___ , ___

g. at, bad, cats, _____ , _____

The look-for-a-pattern strategy is used to ascertain a regular, systematic repetition. Once a pattern has been identified, it is easy to predict what comes next. Most of the patterns dealt with will be numerical in nature, but patterns will also be introduced that deal with words or sounds.

## Problem 1

Students should be asked to look for a pattern that makes some sense — some way to fill in the blank hexagons that works with what is already in place. In this particular problem, the students will soon discover that they cannot apply the same rule for the side-joined hexagons as they can for the vertically-joined hexagons.

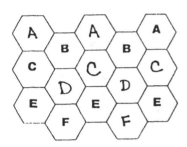

**Answer**: Moving straight down the honeycomb, students will skip every other letter, so that C will follow A, etc. Moving sideways down the honeycomb, letters will follow sequentially in alphabetical order.

## Problem 2

One of the delightful things about this problem is that students will see that mathematical thinking and problem solving skills don't always have to be looked at through a framework of numbers.

Some of the students will recognize that these are patterns involving names in alphabetical order, but the more astute students will also recognize that the numbers of letters within the names have been increasing by one in each successive element.

**Answer**: Answers might be, but are not limited to the following:
- A. David, Danny, or Denny
- B. Martha, Margot, Mitzie, or Mollie.
- C. John, Joel, or Joey

## Problem 3

It is easiest to look for a pattern when the numbers are arranged in a simple format, something like the following:

| Day | 1 | 2 | 3 | 4 |
|---|---|---|---|---|
| Additions | 7 | 8 | 9 | 10 |
| Total | 7 | 15 | 24 | 34 |

When this simple format is used, it is easy to see that the number added each day increases by one, and then continue this pattern to discover the answer.

**Answer**: 84 ladybugs

© Prufrock Press Inc • *No Problem!*

## Problem 4

This problem highlights the Fibonacci sequence, named after the Italian mathematician who discovered the pattern. It is predicated on the simple formula that any number in the sequence is derived from the addition of the two preceding numbers. Many items in nature like legs on a spider, branches on a tree, leaves on a clover, lines on a sea shell, and petals on a rose are Fibonacci numbers. There are entire texts devoted to the study of natural phenomena that occur as Fibonacci numbers.

Once students recognize this pattern, they should easily be able to furnish the next two numbers. For additional challenge, you might want to ask them to find the tenth member of this set.

**Answer**: The next two numbers are 21 and 34.

## Problem 5

These four problems should provide a moderate challenge to children as they do the work of detectives to solve the patterns. Try not to provide too many hints or clues, but encourage students to play with the numbers and delight in the challenge.

The patterns are as follows:
A. add 3, subtract 2
B. 1st, 3rd, 5th, 7th, etc. numbers are related in one pattern, which is add 11. 2nd, 4th, 6th, etc. are related in a separate pattern, which is add 10.
C. multiply by 2, subtract 2
D. subtract 2, add 5

Answer: A. 7, 5
          B. 50, 44
          C. 10, 20
          D. 12, 17

## Bonus Problem

These problems present a variety of patterns, combining both numbers and letters. Students should study the sequences for patterns relating to arithmetic as well as order.

Answer: a. 25, 36 (add progressive odd numbers)
          b. K, L (skip every third letter)
          c. 10, 7 (divide by two and add two)
          d. Q, 7 (every fourth letter beginning at the end of the alphabet, odd numbers)
          e. 32, 64 (add 4, multiple by 2)
          f. 1.0, .8 (add .3, subtract .2)
          g. any 5-letter word beginning with D, any 6-letter word beginning with E

## Problem 1

May B. So showed her cousin, May B. Not, nine cups with numbers on them that had been placed in such a way that there were three cups in each of three stacks. May B. So wanted May B. Not to move only one of the cups so that the sum of the cups in each of the stacks would be equal. Which cup(s) should be moved and to what stack?

## Problem 2

Dom Innow was playing with his favorite game, dominoes. He chose four of the dominoes (those given below) and wondered if they could be arranged in a square so that the sum of all sides would be equal. Show him how this can be done by filling in the correct number of dots on the blank dominoes.

© Prufrock Press Inc • *No Problem!*

## Problem 3

Jim Nasium, the physical education teacher, was working with a group of ten children when the principal, Miss B. Good, walked up behind the group. She asked the children to turn around and then challenged them to see if they could figure out which three children would move (and where) so that they would be in the same arrangement they were in when they were facing Mr. Nasium. Put an X on each child who should move and draw an arrow to their new location.

Jim Nasium

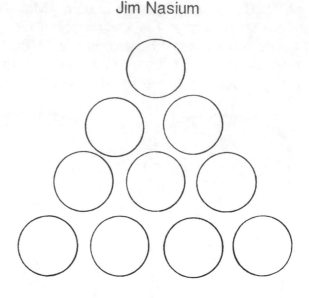

Miss B. Good

## Problem 4

Terry Cloth had 12 toothpicks and six beans that he had arranged like this:

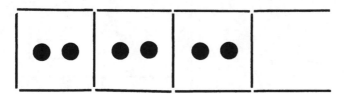

His mother told him to pretend that the beans were sheep and that the toothpicks were sections of fence. Then she challenged him to find a way to give each sheep its own enclosed pen so that all the pens were of equal size. He had to use the exact twelve pieces of fence (no more and no less). Draw a picture of how he should arrange his toothpicks.

# Problem 5

Dee Scovery runs a space shuttle service, transferring cargo from one space station to another. Her assignment is to take three different items (a scientist from another country, film that contains important military information, and a container of radioactive material) from the Beta–Thrust loading dock to Space Station Alpha. She can only take two items in her spaceship at a time. She cannot leave the astronaut and the film alone on the loading dock or on the space station together or the astronaut might steal the secret information. She also cannot leave the film and the radioactive material together in either location or the radioactive material might ruin the film. Figure out a plan for Dee to transport all three items to the space station.

# Bonus Problem

Cliff Hanger is experimenting with bingo chip patterns on his desk top. First he makes a small triangle using only 3 chips. By adding one more row of chips he can make another triangle, this time using a total of 6 chips. The third equilateral triangle that he can make requires 10 chips. If he continues adding one row of chips each time to make the next triangular arrangement, how many chips will he need for his tenth triangle?

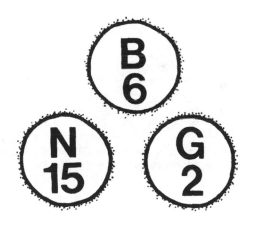

© Prufrock Press Inc • *No Problem!*

Acting things out or using manipulatives is a helpful strategy for those students who have an easier time solving a problem when they can visualize either the data or the process. Sometimes the objects used will be the actual ones needed (as with toothpicks), but often they will be representations of the actual objects (scraps of paper or material substitutions). Sometimes it is helpful to act out a simpler version of the problem in order to visualize the process that is involved before tackling the actual problem.

## Problem 1

Students will have an easy time solving this problem once they have made representations of the nine stacking cups with nine small pieces of scratch paper numbered 2 through 10. Hints you can give the students that won't give away the answer are to add up each stack to see what the sums are before trying to move one cup or to determine what the sums of each stack must be by finding one third the sum of all the cups.

**Answer**: The number 9 stacking cup should move to the first stack.

## Problem 2

Once again, pieces of scrap paper used as representations of the four dominoes will be helpful in solving this problem. Students should be encouraged to enjoy the challenge of being problem solving detectives.

**Answer**: Turned in any way that has these combinations, the arrangement is:

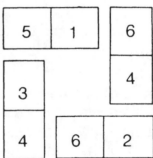

## Problem 3

Bingo chips, scraps of paper, pennies, or any manipulative that makes sense to the children will be helpful in solving this classic problem.

**Answer**:

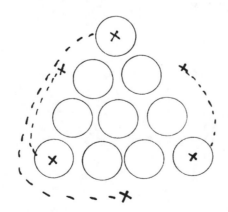

# Problem 4

The solution to this problem requires that children break mindsets and think in new ways about the possibilities of penning the sheep. If students are really puzzled (which is very possible), you might want to go through a brainstorming session with them about the closed geometric shapes that can be made with toothpicks. You may wish to give students a hint by telling them that the sections of fence may be moved into a different shape and then the sheep can be moved into the pens. In other words, they do not have to build the fence around the sheep in their present positions.

**Answer:**

# Problem 5

Although this problem is different from previous problems, this one also lends itself to solving by use of manipulatives. Students might have an easier time if they have four different colored scraps of paper (one for Dee, one for the astronaut, one for the film, and one for the radioactive material) that they can maneuver to find the best solution.

This is a problem that is appropriate for solving in small groups, allowing students an opportunity to share their thought processes and to brainstorm solutions. If small groups are used, make sure each group is comprised of several ability levels.

**Answer:** Trip 1 – Take film to space station
Trip 2 – Take astronaut to space station, bring back film to loading dock
Trip 3 – Take radioactive material to space station, leave material with the astronaut
Trip 4 – Take film to space station

# Bonus Problem

Students may want to solve this problem by actually creating triangles using chips or other manipulatives. They may also draw the triangles. More advanced students may be able to see a pattern and project, based on this pattern, how many chips the tenth triangle will need.

**Answer:** Cliff will need 66 chips for the tenth triangle.

© Prufrock Press Inc · *No Problem!*

## Problem 1

Willy, Milly, Billy, and Lily (all members of the Silly family) each decided to order a different kind of pancake at the restaurant. The four choices were apple, chocolate chip, blueberry, and spice. Using the following clues, who ordered which pancakes?

**Clues**

1. Willy hates apple.
2. Milly is allergic to chocolate.
3. The girls didn't order anything with fruit.

## Problem 2

I. D. Solver has five pictures in front of him and needs to figure out the identities based on only three clues. He might not be able to do it, but you sure can! After reading the three clues, determine who is Ugg, Mug, Wug, Slug, and Thug.

**Clues**

1. Ugg and Mug are smiling.
2. Ugg and Thug have big eyes.
3. Slug has a big nose.

## Problem 3

Bea Smart has six papers with grades of A, B, C, D, F, and Incomplete on them. She has put them in two separate piles. She put the paper graded with a B directly under the paper with a C grade. She put the incomplete paper to the right of the B paper, but not on top. She put the paper graded with a D on top of the paper with a C. At the end, Bea put the F paper between the A and the incomplete paper. Figure out which paper is in which position and put the correct grade on each piece of paper.

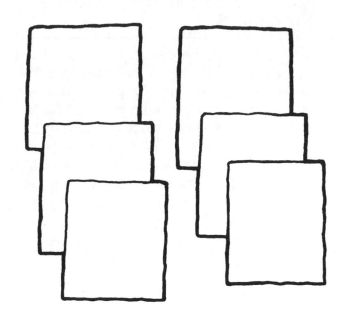

## Problem 4

Stu Dent has six books all in a row on his bookshelf for his classes in math, science, history, spelling, art, and reading. Read the clues and label the books correctly.

### Clues
1. The math book is to the left of the science and history books.
2. The science and spelling books are on the two ends.
3. The art and the history books occupy the two center positions.
4. The reading book is in between the history and science books.

© Prufrock Press Inc • *No Problem!*

## Problem 5

Below is the basic floor plan of the five connected stores that make up the Buy-A-Lot Shopping Center. Each store is shown with windows indicated by a thick, dark line and doors indicated by two parallel slashes in the front wall of the plan. After reading the clues, write the type of store in the correct space.

**Clues**

1. The jewelry store has a side window.
2. The video store is between the drug store and the beauty parlor.
3. The drug store is next to the jewelry store.
4. The real estate office has windows in front and on the right.

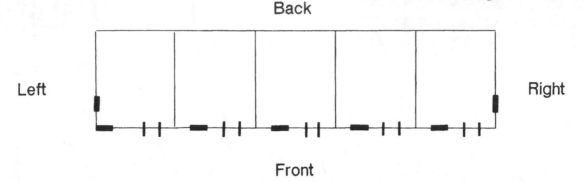

## Bonus Problem

Four friends, Ellie, Tim, Faye, and Joe, sat at a table for lunch. Each was wearing a different color (green, red, yellow, and blue) and each ordered a different kind of sandwich (cheese, ham, tuna, and peanut butter). Using the clues, find out who sat in each seat, what color each person was wearing, and what kind of sandwich each had to eat.

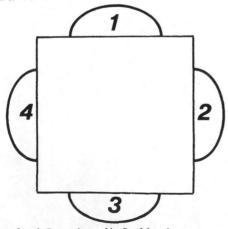

**Clues**

1. The person in green sat opposite the person in blue, who had a cheese sandwich.

2. The person in red was not sitting in seat 3 or 4.

3. Tim sat in an odd numbered seat, opposite the person with the ham sandwich.

4. The person in seat 2 ate tuna and wore green. This wasn't Ellie, who wore red.

5. Faye sat in seat 4.

The ability to use logical reasoning is a prerequisite to solving many types of math problems. While logical thinking has a broad application, mathematics provides an excellent discipline for learning logical structures. It is useful, therefore, to teach it as a separate problem solving strategy. This strategy is especially useful when there are conditional statements and answers that are dependent on other answers (such as; *if this is true, then this statement must also be true*). Instruction in logical thinking should include problems that develop reasoning patterns and also present applications of reasoning patterns to both mathematical and non-mathematical situations.

## Problem 1

Students might have an easier time understanding how to use the clues if you show them how to use a grid similar to the one below.

|       | apple | chocolate | blueberry | spice |
|-------|-------|-----------|-----------|-------|
| Willy | no    |           |           |       |
| Milly | no    | no        |           |       |
| Billy |       |           |           |       |
| Lily  | no    |           |           |       |

**Answer**: Willy – blueberry
Milly – spice
Billy – apple
Lily – chocolate chip

## Problem 2

Rather than the grid, students might want to use the picture to eliminate the possibilities according to the clues. One way to do this is to put all five initials above each face. After reading each clue, students can cross out the initials that need to be eliminated. For instance, after reading the first clue, students would cross off the U and M above the 3rd, 4th, and 5th faces.

**Answer**: 1st – Ugg        4th – Wug
2nd – Mug       5th – Slug
3rd – Thug

## Problem 3

This problem can be solved with manipulatives, but logical thinking is still a part of the process. Six scraps of paper can represent the six papers that Bea Smart has placed in two stacks. Manipulation and thinking should make this a fairly easy problem.

**Answer**: From top to bottom, the papers are:
Left stack – D, C, B
Right stack – A, F, Incomplete

© Prufrock Press Inc • *No Problem!*

## Problem 4

Students might attack this problem in one of two ways. First, they might use six pieces of scrap paper labeled as the books and manipulate those representations according to the given clues. They also might put letters representing the choices above each of the books and cross off those that are eliminated by the clues. You might want to present both methodological choices to students.

**Answer**: (from left to right): spelling, math, art, history, reading, science

## Problem 5

The easiest way for the students to solve this problem is to sketch a quick diagram across the top of a sheet of scratch paper and label that sketch as the clues are presented. Clues one and four will give students the start they need to solve the entire problem.

**Answer**: From left to right, the stores are:
jewelry, drug store, video, beauty parlor, real estate

## Bonus Problem

Students will need to make a grid that contains all the information presented in this problem (names, colors, positions, and sandwiches). As clues are given, they can mark positive and negative identifications on the grid. Students must use deductive reasoning for some of the clues. For instance, clue three tells them that Tim did not eat ham and did not sit in seat 2 or 4.

**Answer**:  seat 1 – Ellie, red, ham
seat 2 – Joe, green, tuna
seat 3 – Tim, yellow, peanut butter
seat 4 – Faye, blue, cheese

## Problem 1

Frank Lee needed one and a half gallons of soda pop for a party. When he went to the Stop 'n Shop Market, he found three different sizes of soda pop. He could buy one–half gallon for $1.92, 12–ounce cans for 40¢ each, or a package of six 16–ounce bottles for $4.80. Determine how many of each container Frank needs in order to make one and a half gallons and what size of container will give Frank what he needs at the best price?

Hint: There are 128 fluid ounces in a gallon.

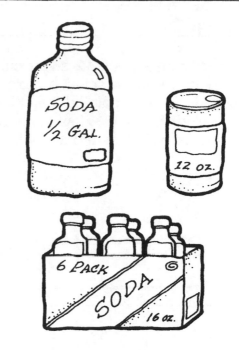

## Problem 2

Teacher, Hope Springs, entered the Eternal Preschool at 8 a.m. on a Monday morning just in time to witness what turned out to be a flu epidemic at the school. By 8:30 a.m., half the children were sent home sick. By 9:30 a.m., half of the remaining children were sent home. By 10:30 a.m., half of the remaining children were sent home. By 11:30 a.m., half of the remaining children were sent home. By that time it was lunchtime and there were only two children left. How many students were in the class at the beginning of the day?

37

## Problem 3

Char Treuse glued 12 sugar cubes together into a long strip for a science project. After the glue dried, she painted the entire strip a pretty color of green. How many sides of sugar cubes were painted altogether?

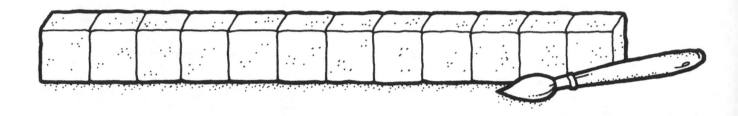

## Problem 4

It was snack time for Mo and Flo Gno at Mrs. Pasture's Cookie Shop. They were trying to decide what kinds of cookies they wanted. In the counter there were 6 more chocolate mint cookies than white frosted cookies, but the sum of the mint and frosted was equal to the total of peanut butter cookies. They saw exactly twice as many peanut butter cookies as oatmeal cookies. There were one third as many peanut butter as chocolate chip, and their mouths were watering looking at the 36 chocolate chip cookies. How many cookies were there in the shop?

_____ chocolate chip

_____ chocolate mint

_____ oatmeal

_____ peanut butter

_____ white frosted

_____ total number of cookies

## Problem 5

The Bread brothers, Ed, Fred, Ned, Jed, Red, and Ted, were competing against each other to see who could build the tallest tower using wooden blocks. Ed finished his tower first. Fred built a tower that was 4 blocks taller that Ed's. Ned built a tower 4 blocks taller than Fred's. Jed's tower was 4 blocks taller than Ned's, and Red's was 4 blocks taller than Jed's. Finally, Ted topped them all with a tower 32 blocks high, which was 4 blocks taller than Red's tower. How many blocks were used altogether by the Bread brothers to build their towers?

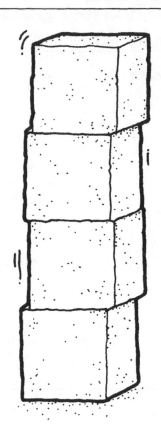

## Bonus Problem

Twenty-four (24) students are in Miss Favor's class. One sixth (1/6) of the students were born in the first quarter of the year. One half (1/2) of the remaining students were born in April. One half (1/2) of the remaining students were born in the months of May through August. There are no September birthdays, but one fifth (1/5) of the remaining birthdays are in October. If 1 student was born in November, how many December birthdays are there?

© Prufrock Press Inc • *No Problem!*

Simplifying the problem is a useful strategy when there is an abundance of data or data that is presented in multiple formats. Sometimes there is a need to simplify a problem by working backwards, looking at the end of the problem instead of at the beginning.

## Problem 1

This problem demonstrates the make-it-simpler methodology as students find out that the easiest way to solve the problem is to first find out how many ounces will be needed to make one and one-half gallons (192 ounces). Then students will determine how many units are needed to make 192 ounces for each of the three different packages. They will find that they need three half-gallon containers, 16 of the 12-ounce cans, and two of the six-packs. Then students will find the cost for each of these purchases by multiplying the cost times the number of units needed. Finally, students will determine the best value. In order to work this problem, students need to know that there are 128 fluid ounces in a gallon.

**Answer**: Three half-gallon containers give the needed 192 ounces for $5.76. This is the best value.
Sixteen (16) cans will cost $6.40.
Two cases of bottles will cost $9.60.

## Problem 2

This is an excellent problem to demonstrate the effectiveness of working backwards to solve a problem. In this particular problem, the students will start at the end with two students left by lunchtime. With two students left at lunch, there had to be four students left at 11:30 a.m. and 8 students left at 10:30 a.m. Continuing this process, students will double the amount of students each hour until they get to the answer of 32 students.

**Answer**: 32 students

## Problem 3

This example of a make-it-simpler problem also combines the strategies learned earlier of making a table and looking for a pattern. Students will simplify the problem by first determining how many sides are painted on a single cube, and then on a double, etc. The listing below shows the number of cubes on the top and the number of painted sides directly underneath. They also could figure that there are 12 squares on each of the four sides of the chain (total 48 squares) plus the two end squares.

| cubes | 1 | 2 | 3 | 4 | 5 | 6 |
|-------|---|----|----|----|----|----|
| sides | 6 | 10 | 14 | 18 | 22 | 26 |

**Answer**: 50 painted sides

# Problem 4

This problem also requires students to work backwards, going to the end of the problem and working from the given number of 36 chocolate chip cookies, and also to use logical thinking. With 36 chocolate chip, there had to be 12 peanut butter and another 12 in a combination of chocolate mint and white frosted. Since there were six more chocolate mint than white frosted, there had to be 9 chocolate mint and 3 white frosted. There were twice as many peanut butter as oatmeal, so there were 6 oatmeal cookies.

Students should list exactly how many of each type of cookie as a way to check the problem and prove the answer.

**Answer**: chocolate chip      36
peanut butter      12
chocolate mint     9
white frosted      3
oatmeal      6

Total      66 cookies

# Problem 5

Once again, students will have a chance to work backwards, starting with the last piece of information in the problem, 32 blocks in Ted's tower. If Ted's tower had 32, then Red's tower had 28, Jed's tower had 24, Ned's tower had 20, Fred's tower has 16, and Ed's smallest tower had 12 blocks.

**Answer**: 132 blocks altogether

# Bonus Problem

In this problem, students need to make a series of calculations. They can start with the fact that there are 24 students in the class and begin by finding 1/6 of this amount for the first set of birthdays. They should then make note of the fact that 4 of the birthdays fall between January and March, leaving 20 birthdays for the rest of the year. In a similar fashion, they should continue figuring the birthdays for each month and subtracting that number from the total number of birthdays remaining.

**Answer**:   4 birthdays – January – March
10 birthdays – April
5 birthdays – May – August
1 birthday – October
1 birthday – November
3 birthdays – December

41

## Problem 1

Lady Bug lives in the southwest corner of a garden that is 12 feet by 10 feet. The garden is surrounded by a sidewalk that is 2 feet wide. Each day she takes a walk, following the same route. She walks around the perimeter of the garden, crosses the sidewalk and then walks the outside perimeter of the sidewalk and finally walks back across the sidewalk (at the same place she originally crossed the sidewalk) to her home. How many feet does she travel during her walk each day?

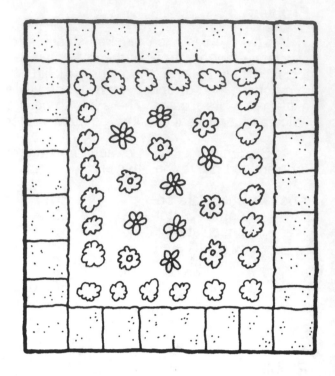

## Problem 2

Fred T. Croaker, a very clumsy frog, fell down an old abandoned well. The well was 20 feet deep and the sides were slick and hard to climb. It was 8 a.m. when Fred started climbing up. Each hour he climbed up 3 feet before sliding back down 1 foot. At this rate, at what time did Fred finally climb out of the well?

# Problem 3

The playground at Learnalot School has large circles painted in a straight line from one side of the playground to the other side. Ann T. Social is playing a game of tag with her friends. She is standing in a circle near the middle of the playground and doesn't want to get caught on her way to join her friends, Carrie Deway and Dee Litefull, who are waiting in another circle. She runs three circles east before running back four circles to the west. She is able to make a mad dash five circle to the east before racing to the last circle west of her, which is eight circles away. Slowly she runs two circles east and then two more circles east. Carrie and Dee are waiting for her four circles to the east, so she then joins them. Ann quickly leaves her friends and starts for the last circle, which is one more circle to the east, when she is caught by Steve Ador, her arch enemy. How many circles are there altogether?

# Problem 4

Minnie Sota and Ken Tucky were getting directions from Al Abama on how to get from the State of Confusion to the State of Bliss. Al told them to proceed four miles straight north, walk three miles straight east, go exactly two miles further north, turn to the west and continue for six miles, go south only one mile, and then east one more mile. He told them to conclude the journey by going five miles north. Make a map for Minnie and Ken to the State of Bliss using Al's directions.

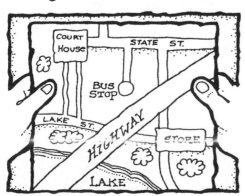

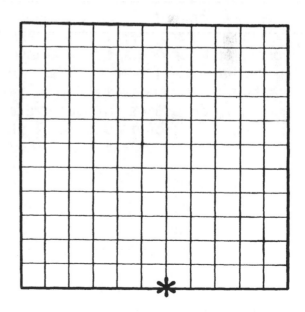

© Prufrock Press Inc • *No Problem!*

## Problem 5

Room 12's pet mouse, Mickey, was in the school hallway trying to find a discarded piece of cheese by reading the directions given to him earlier that day by the pet gerbil. The instructions told the young mouse to start at the southeast corner and walk north one floor tile and then west one tile. Then go seven floor tiles north followed by three tiles to the west. The next directions looked like this:

    one tile southeast
    three tiles west
    two tiles southeast
    three tiles southwest
    and nine tiles north.

Use graph paper and map out the path for the bewildered mouse. Give directions for a more direct path to the cheese.

## Bonus Problem

In the kingdom of Ancient Times, the telephone hookups do not go through a central location. Instead, any hut that wants to be connected to any other hut must have a direct line to that hut. If there are 5 huts, each wanting to be connected with all of the other 4 huts, how many lines are needed altogether? If five more huts are added to the kingdom, how many telephone lines will be required?

Making a diagram or drawing is a particularly useful strategy for solving problems that can be illustrated. Sometimes graph paper is helpful and should be available for the students. Usually it is not the preciseness of the drawing that makes the difference; the solving occurs when children are able to work with the data in a concrete way that makes sense to each of them.

## Problem 1

This problem is quite easy if students draw a picture of the garden that looks like the following. They can then add the perimeter of the garden (44 feet) plus the perimeter of the sidewalk (60 feet) plus twice the width of the sidewalk (4 feet).

**Answer**: She travels 108 feet.

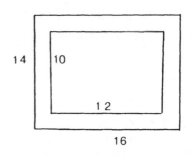

## Problem 2

Students will have an easier time solving this problem if they use quadrille paper with 20 squares or draw a vertical line with small horizontal marks to represent 20 one-foot segments. Students should chart the frog's progress by drawing a line up three units and then down one unit for each hour that passes. In this way they will conceptually understand the problem and arrive at the accurate answer.

**Answer**: Fred will climb out sometime between 5:00 and 6:00 p.m.

## Problem 3

This is a good problem to read aloud. It is recommended that you read the story through once and then discuss some parts of the problem and strategies that will be helpful for students. For instance, hopefully some of the students will have heard that Ann was standing near the center of the playground. This would indicate that they should draw their first circle in the middle of the paper. Predictions of what the total number of circles will be should help students know about what size the circles can be to fit across their paper. After this initial discussion, slowly read the problem to the students and have them draw the circles as you read the clues.

**Answer**: 10 circles

45

## Problem 4

Students will need quadrille paper and a starting point near the bottom center of their map. They will then work slowly, solving the problem by drawing the diagram or the map.

**Answer:** A more direct route would be to go north 10 miles and west 2 miles.

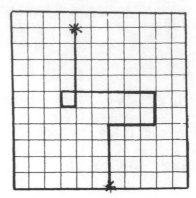

## Problem 5

Like the previous problem, students will need to read carefully in order to draw a map. The difference in this problem is that it adds the dimension of combined directions like southeast. Give your students a starting point near the southeast corner of their paper, as per the gerbil's directions.

**Answer:** A more direct route would be 11 tiles north and 7 tiles west.

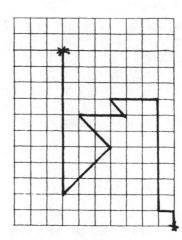

## Bonus Problem

Students will be able to solve this problem easily if they draw a picture of five huts and trace out the connections for each hut, remembering that there only needs to be one line between each hut. They should see that the first hut has 4 lines, the second hut has 3 additional lines, the third hut has 2 additional lines, the fourth hut has 1 additional line, making a total of 10 lines. They can use the same logic or strategy to solve the problem for 10 huts without having to draw a picture.

**Answer:** Five huts need 10 lines.
Ten huts need 45 lines.

The problems for the rest of the year are presented so you can write them on the board or duplicate them for student use. Answers for each of the problems are in a separate appendix at the end of the book. Another item in the appendix that should be of use is the student recording sheet. Utilizing these sheets will force students to show their chosen strategy(ies) and all of the problem solving steps they went through. The problems are mixed according to the types of strategies that are necessary so that students are forced to choose how they will solve each problem. There is not always one correct strategy choice; different students and different groups might opt for alternative ways of attacking problems, all of which are perfectly acceptable. What matters most is that an atmosphere supportive of problem solving is provided for students — one where risk-taking is encouraged and rewarded. When that supportive atmosphere is present, students are far more likely to spend time thinking, reasoning, and stretching themselves to new limits and make greater use of their abilities.

## Problem 49

Billy Club was assigned the task of putting numbers on all of the playground balls used during daily recess. Billy will number the balls using the following rules:

**Rules**
1. It will be a 4-digit number.
2. The digit in the thousands place will be a 1 or a 2.
3. The digit in the hundreds place will be a 2, 4, or 6.
4. The digit in the tens place will be an odd number.
5. The digit in the ones place will be greater than six.

How many balls can Billy number if he follows these rules?

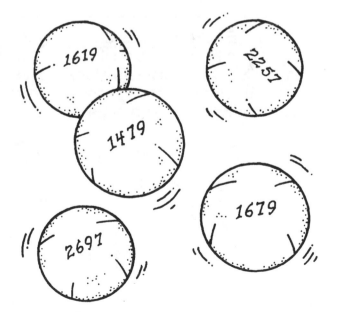

© Prufrock Press Inc • *No Problem!*

## Problem 50

Warren Tee, the local car dealer, had trouble remembering where his cars were parked. He decided to keep a chart and number his parking spaces. Unfortunately, his friend, the painter Will B. Strate, could only paint straight lines. This meant that he could only number the spaces with the numerals 1, 4, and 7. The spaces all had 3-digit numbers (like 111 or 114). How many parking spaces could he make?

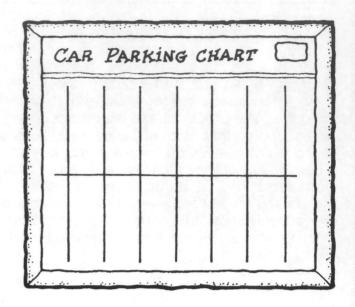

## Problem 51

Gail E. Dunn was assigned the task of stacking bolts of material in the fabric store. She had 6 bolts to stack. She put the black print material between the white material and the orange.

She put the red material on the left end, right next to the white. She put the plaid material between the orange and the yellow. Can you fill in the color of each?

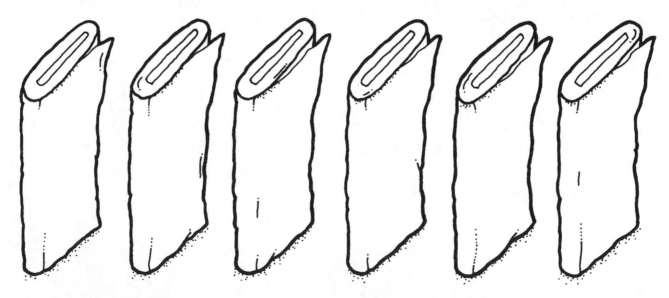

## Problem 52

Wanda Myway, the spoiled rich girl, couldn't make up her mind what kind of car her father should buy for her. She wanted a sports car but couldn't decide whether it should be bottle green or silver and whether it should be a convertible or sun-roof. She also couldn't decide whether it should be a Porsche, Jaguar, or a Corvette. With these choices, what are all the different cars that Wanda could order?

## Problem 53

Two best friends and tent-mates at camp, Earl E. Toobed and Earl E. Toorise, liked to play practical jokes on their friends before they got up each morning. On the first day they put a frog in the tent 4 tents north of theirs. The next morning they poured ice water under the flap of the tent 2 tents to the south. The next morning they found their friend Bob White's tent, 5 tents to the north, and hid his underwear. Bob decided to join in on the pranks and put ants in the tent at the end of the row, 2 tents north of his. Earl E. Toobed and Earl E. Toorise got caught trying to sew the counselor into his tent at the beginning of the row, 6 tents to the south of theirs. How many tents were in line at the camp?

© Prufrock Press Inc • No Problem!

## Problem 54

Vick Tory is hooked on his new Nonbendo Game. The first day he can only get through level 1 of the first world. The next day he gets through level 3. The next day he makes it to the 7th level, having conquered two more levels than he had the day before. The fourth day he makes it to level 13. If each succeeding day he conquers two more levels than he has the previous day, on what day will he rescue the princess at the 32nd level?

## Problem 55

Carol Stream wanted to get back to her camp on the other side of the woods. She could either take the north path over the logs, the middle path that ran next to the creek or the south path through the orchard. All three paths met about 100 yards east of the creek. She could then cross the regular bridge over the creek, use the stepping stones across the creek, or swing on a vine across the creek. Then Carol could choose the bridle path into camp or the footpath. How many possible ways are there for Carol to get back to camp?

## Problem 56

Barb R. Pole has a collection of hair decorations. She sorts her barrettes and ribbons and has a total of 65 items. She has 17 more barrettes than ribbons. How many of each does she have?

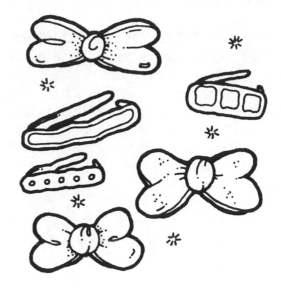

## Problem 57

Matt Tress found 46 cents under his bed. He had less than 11 coins and one of the coins was a quarter. What are the combinations of coins he could have?

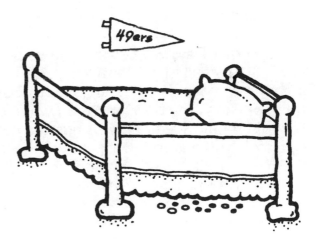

© Prufrock Press Inc • *No Problem!*

## Problem 58

Pat T. Melt and Max E. Mum are building giant submarine sandwiches for a party. Max started first and already has 11 pieces of cold cuts on his creation. Pat only has 2 on hers. If they continue together, each adding a slice at the same time, Max's sandwich will soon have exactly twice the number of slices as Pat's. How many slices of cold cuts will Max's sandwich have then?

## Problem 59

Summer Days will be traveling with her family to a small island for a vacation. They are trying to decide whether to go by bus, train, or car to the dock and then whether to rent a boat, ride a ferry, or ride the new hydrofoil to the island. Once on the island they can backpack, ride horseback, or bike to their cottage. How many different combinations can Summer and her family use to travel from their home to the island?

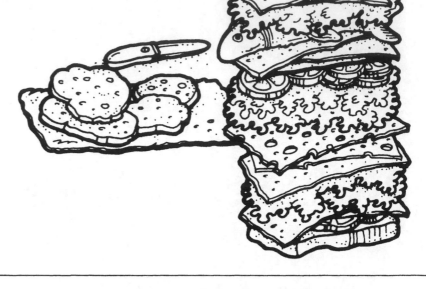

## Problem 60

Al E. Bye and Paul Tree decided to have a contest to see which one of them could earn and save $100.00 first. They mowed lawns and did chores, and at the end of the first day, Al had $3.00 and Paul had $9.00. At the end of the second day, Al had $6.00 and Paul had $18.00. At the end of the third day, Al had $12.00 and Paul had $27.00. At the close of the fourth day, Al had $24.00 and Paul had $36.00. At this rate, who will win the contest and how many days will it take?

## Problem 61

Cassie O. Pia is doing a science project on ancient constellation figures. She is using star stickers to show the configurations. She is showing only the stars above the 4th magnitude in each constellation. There are 6 more stars in Leo than in Aries. Centaurus, with 14 stars, has 4 stars more than Leo but 3 less than Scorpio. How many stars does she need for each constellation?

53

© Prufrock Press Inc • No Problem!

## Problem 62

Sue S. Canal docks her motorboat at pier one. Six boats use the pier, three tied to each side. Each boat on the pier is a different color. Sue's boat is white and is directly across the pier from the green boat. The green boat is between the silver boat and the blue boat. The yellow boat is west of hers, and the silver boat is exactly north of the red boat. Where is each boat tied up?

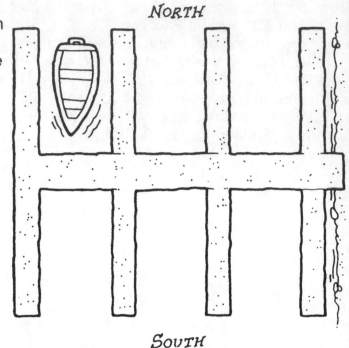

## Problem 63

Willy Makeitt, the carpenter, was paid $30.00 for each chair and $50.00 for each table he built. At the end of one week he had earned $410.00. How many chairs did he make and how many tables?

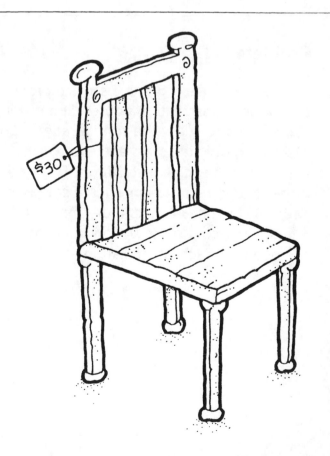

## Problem 64

Ken L. Man worked for the Happy Hound Animal Clinic. When he started, he earned $20.00 per day. He soon had a raise to $29.00 per day. This raise was $1.50 per hour. How many hours per day was he working?

## Problem 65

The Chicago Bears beat the New York Giants in the Super Bowl by a score of 24 — 0. Use the scoring guide below to figure out all the different scoring possibilities if there were no 2-point conversions.

Scoring is as follows:
    touchdown - 6 points
    point after touchdown - 1 point
    safety - 2 points
    field goal - 3 points

© Prufrock Press Inc • No Problem!

## Problem 66

Molly, Polly, and Dolly Folly all want to play by themselves with a single friend in a different part of the house. They can play in the bedroom, dining room, or family room. Four toys are available — a doll, a book, a train, and a puzzle. Five friends might come over — Jan, Jen, Jinx, Joan, or June. How many different possibilities are there?

## Problem 67

The fourth grade at Knowledge School decided to graph the favorite colors of all the children in their school. If they graph 15 names the first day and increase that number by 5 each day (so that they add 20 on the second day, 25 on the third day, etc.), how many days will it take to finish the graph of 512 students?

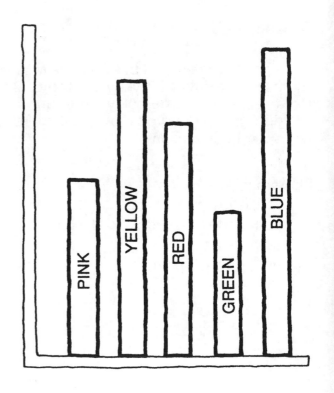

## Problem 68

Two hundred ten (210) people went swimming at the local pool. Thirty (30) people spent time in both the shallow and deep ends, but of the remaining people, Wade Deep, the lifeguard, reported that twice as many people swam in the deep end as those that stayed in the shallow end. How many people swam only in the shallow end? How many people swam only in the deep end?

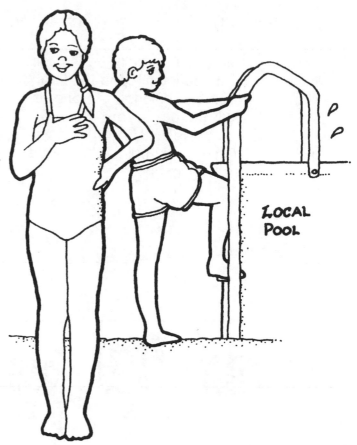

## Problem 69

Chip Endale has a favorite number. Use the following clues to figure out what his favorite number is.

- The number is greater than 8 x 6.
- The number is odd.
- The number is less that 9 x 8.
- One of the factors of the number is 3.
- 5 is not one of the digits.
- The numeral in the ten's place is smaller than the numeral in the one's place.

© Prufrock Press Inc · *No Problem!*

## Problem 70

Six glasses of partially consumed juice sat on the counter top in the Bran's kitchen. Each one belonged to one of the Bran children, Jan, Van, Dan, Fran, Stan, and Nan. Using these clues, determine which glass belonged to each of the six Bran children.

### Clues

1. Jan drank about half of her juice.
2. Two of the girls had the end glasses.
3. Van is a boy and Jan is a girl.
4. None of the boys drank half a glass of juice.
5. Van and Dan barely drank any of their juice.
6. Stan and Fran drank the most.
7. Van had glass E.

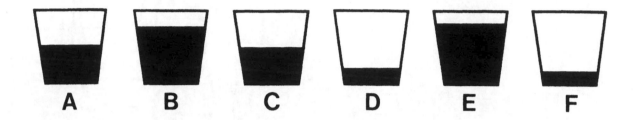

---

## Problem 71

Continue this pattern that was started by Jack B. Nimbell.

| | | | | | |
|---|---|---|---|---|---|
| △ | ◆ | ○ | ★ | △ | ◆ |
| ◆ | ○ | ★ | △ | ◆ | ○ |
| ○ | ★ | △ | ◆ | | |
| | | | | | |
| | | | | | |

## Problem 72

Darlene and Marlene live in houses with trees on only one side. Carleen and Darlene have fireplaces. Sharlene has the least number of windows. Where does each girl live?

## Problem 73

Mrs. Chris N. Ing is trying to plan her baby's baptism party. She has made a guest list of 32 names. Her mother-in-law gives her a list of 28 names to add to the guest list. Upon checking, she finds that 12 of their friends are the same. How many invitations does she need?

© Prufrock Press Inc • No Problem!

## Problem 74

Luke Warm and Sandy Beach were collecting sea shells along the coast. They found 99 shells. They had 25 more scallop shells than conch shells. How many of each kind of shell did they have?

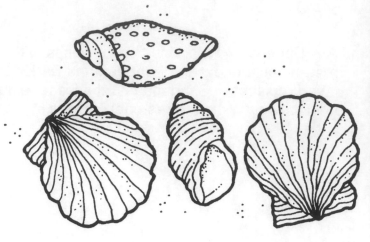

## Problem 75

Justin A. Bank puts 1 penny in a jar on Monday, 2 pennies in the jar on Tuesday, 4 pennies on Wednesday and continues to double the number of pennies each day. How many pennies will be in the jar on Friday of the second week?

# Problem 76

Iva Numeral loves the number 21. She wants to put one-digit numbers on the three birdhouses in her yard so that the sum of the three numbers used totals 21. If she doesn't use zero and uses different numbers on all three birdhouses, how many combinations are possible?

# Problem 77

N. Vince Able challenges you to guess his favorite numbers by using these three clues:

- Each number is a four-digit odd number.
- Each is a palindrome (reads the same backwards and forward).
- The digits of each number add up to 10.
- Neither of the numbers is divisible by 5.

© Prufrock Press Inc • *No Problem!*

## Problem 78

Lynn A Mint, the aerobics instructor, had her classes doing calisthenics at a regular pace. The first 5 minutes they did 30 knee-bends, the second 5 minutes included 25 twists, and the third 5 minutes included 27 sit-ups. The fourth 5 minutes they did 22 toe-touches, and in the final 5-minute period, they did 24 high-steps. At this rate, how many actual exercises will the students have done at the end of the 45-minute exercise period if they repeat the same schedule until the end of class.

## Problem 79

The monsters in Fangville were multiplying like crazy. On the first day that Harry Legs counted, there were 33 monsters. On the second day he counted, there were 40 monsters. On the third day, there were 42, and there were 49 monsters on the fourth day. If this pattern continues, how many monsters will be counted on the tenth day?

## Problem 80

Vic Timms and his friends decide to go exploring in the haunted house at the end of Phantom Lane. The house used to belong to Granny Canyon, but it is haunted now. Vic has a choice of 3 different gates to go through, 3 different outside doors, 2 staircases to the second floor, and 2 different staircases to the attic. How many different ways are there for Vic and his friends to get from the street to the attic?

## Problem 81

Mr. and Mrs. Rick O'Shay and their three children paid $105.00 for tickets to an amusement park. If a single child's ticket was one-half of an adult's ticket, how much did the tickets cost?

63

## Problem 82

Seven parrots were sitting in the same tree. The parrots names were Polly, Patty, Penny, Percy, Perry, Pinky, and Peppy. Use the clues below to figure out which parrot sat on which branch.

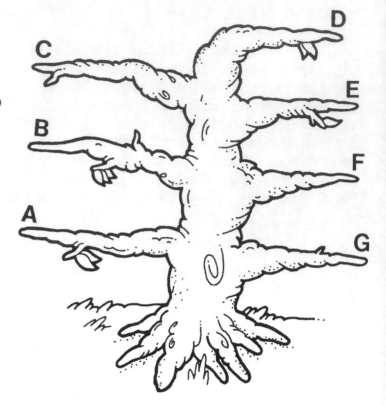

**Clues**
1. The three girls were on one side of the tree.
2. Polly was above Patty and directly to the left of Perry.
3. Penny and Percy occupied the bottom branches.
4. Peppy was alone at the top.

## Problem 83

Willie Dew is a contestant on the Quiz Show, "Don't Guess." Ten points are given for every right answer, and 25 points are deducted for every wrong answer. At the end of the first round, Willie has 65 points after 3 wrong answers. How many correct responses has Willie given?

## Problem 84

Three friends were eating cookies. Chip and Van each ate at least one cookie. Ginger ate the most cookies, but she ate less than 10 cookies. Chip and Van ate the same number of cookies. The product of the three amounts was 12. How many cookies did each cookie muncher eat?

## Problem 85

Joy Ofliving hàs a special game played with pewter and lead pieces. The pewter pieces weigh 17 ounces each and the lead pieces weigh 19 ounces each. All of Joyce's pieces weigh 193 ounces. How many lead pieces and how many pewter pieces does she have?

© Prufrock Press Inc · *No Problem!*

## Problem 86

A bag of gumballs contains 24 gumballs. How many bags would Kent Chew need to buy to make sure that he had one gumball each day for an entire year (not a leap year)? This does not include Sundays, of course, when Kent isn't allowed to chew gum.

## Problem 87

Amy Able needs help figuring out the following problem. Write one of each of the fractions 1/12, 2/12, 3/12, 4/12, 5/12, and 6/12 in each circle so that the sum of any line is 1 (one).

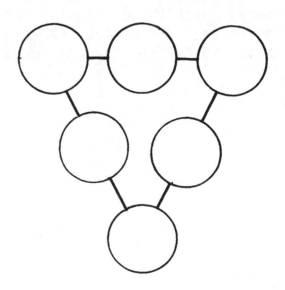

## Problem 88

Lisa Lott and Sy Ninfront both work for Sturdy and Standwell Real Estate. Lisa works every Saturday and Sy comes in and checks the listings every 5 days. They are together today. How many weeks will it be until they see each other at the office again? Their office is open seven days a week.

## Problem 89

Anita Toy has earned bonus points from her teacher for good behavior and grades. These points can be spent on prizes. Anita has 32 bonus points to spend on any of the following:

| | |
|---|---|
| notepads | 10 points |
| pencils | 5 points |
| stickers | 1 point |

How many different combinations of prizes can Anita buy with her 32 points?

© Prufrock Press Inc • No Problem!

## Problem 90

Candy Cane has to put six jars of goodies back on the shelves. She knows that one jar goes on each shelf. Use the following clues to help Candy Cane decide where to put the licorice sticks, root beer barrels, lemon drops, gumballs, orange slices, and rock candy.

### Clues
1. The root beer barrels and orange slices are on the bottom shelf.
2. The rock candy is on the middle shelf on the right hand side, one shelf lower and to the side of the lemon drops.
3. The lemon drops, gumballs, and root beer barrels are all on the same side.

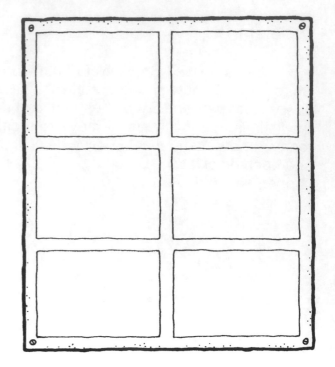

## Problem 91

Bea Steadfast was trying to figure out a number using the following clue: 1/3 of the number is three more than 1/4 of the number. What is the number?

## Problem 92

Pat Tronize was teasing Cam Pane that she had twice as many signatures on her nominating petition than Cam had. Together they had 240 signatures. How many signatures did Pat have? How many signatures did Cam have?

## Problem 93

Mrs. Em Broider loved to make quilts. Her first quilt was 4 squares by 6 squares, made for a baby bed. Her next quilt was 6 squares by 8 squares. Her third quilt was 8 squares by 10 squares. Now she is working on her sixth quilt. Assuming that the pattern has continued, how many squares will be in this quilt?

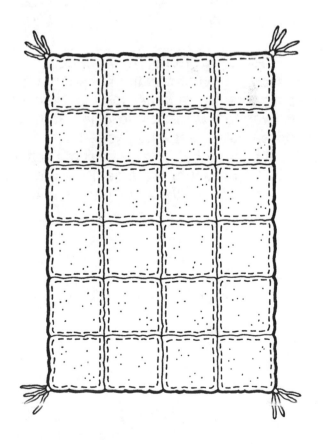

© Prufrock Press Inc · *No Problem!*

## Problem 94

Jan, Dan, Fran, and Nan went to the Barkalot Pet Store. They each bought a pet. The four pets included a Siamese cat, a tabby cat, a German shepherd, and a beagle. Fran always wanted a smaller dog, but Jan and Nan don't like dogs. Jan could only afford the cute tabby cat. Which pet did each child buy?

## Problem 95

Hiram N. Fyrum runs an employment agency. He has three times as many applicants for gardener jobs as he does for dishwasher jobs and two times as many applicants for secretary jobs than for dishwasher jobs. He has 78 applications for these 3 positions on his desk. How many applications are there for each position?

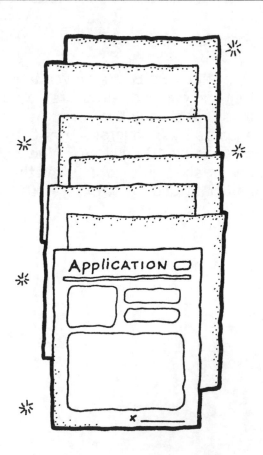

## Problem 96

King Roy L. Tee sponsored a Funfest for his knights who had been getting rusty since the disappearance of dragons. The first event was a long jump in shining armor. Sir Quacky won the event, followed by Sir Lancealittle and Sir Rustedout. Sir Quacky jumped 3 inches farther than Sir Lancealittle after he oiled his armor. Sir Rustedout had a squeaky jump and jumped 6 inches less that Sir Lancealittle. They jumped a total of 51 inches. How far did each knight jump?

## Problem 97

Dwight House wanted to go to Washington, D.C. to see his friend, Phil E. Buster, a congressman. He called his travel agent who told him that he could fly from Midway or O'Hare Airport, that he could leave either airport at 2 p.m., 4 p.m., or 6 p.m., and that there were rooms available in the Hyatt, Marriott, and Sheraton hotels. How many different travel arrangements were possible?

71

© Prufrock Press Inc • No Problem!

## Problem 98

Roger Andout and his friend, Will Coe, want to use their walkie–talkies to give each other directions to their hiding places in the tree nursery. The trees are planted in 12 rows with 12 trees in each row. Roger is in the northwest corner and Will is in the southeast corner. Mark a path for each boy using these clues.

– Roger tells Will to go 5 trees north.
– Will tells Roger to go 3 trees east.
– Roger tells Will to go 4 trees west.
– Will tells Roger to go 5 trees south.
– Roger tells Will to go 2 trees north.
– Will tells Roger to go 4 trees east.

How many trees separate the boys now?

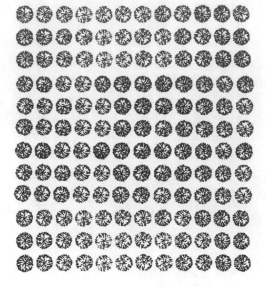

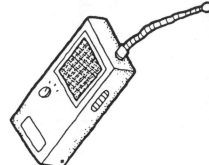

## Problem 99

Mary A. Nett went to the toy store to buy puppets for her summer puppet shows. She wanted to put on a fairy tale puppet show for her friends this year. Dwarf puppets cost $3.00 each, princess puppets cost $6.00 each, and scary witch puppets cost $9.00 each. She had $24.00 saved up to spend on puppets. How many combinations of these puppets were possible for her to purchase with $24.00?

## Problem 100

Mrs. Allie Gator made a home for her six baby alligators in the reeds in the swamp. She divided the area with marshy grasses and made a bed on a lily pad for each of her children, Olly, Molly, Polly, Rolly, Golly and Holly. Their home looked like the drawing to the right. Use the clues to fill in the correct names on the lily pads.

### Clues
1. Olly was ornery so Mrs. Gator kept him right next to her.
2. Molly was between Rolly and Olly.
3. Polly's bed was next to Molly's and closer to her mother than Holly's.

## Problem 101

Professor Phil Osofee did not have enough books for his entire class. His classroom had 30 desks arranged in a giant horseshoe. He put the 10 blue books on every 3rd seat starting with the 3rd seat on the left. He put the 15 red books on every other seat, starting with the second seat. He noticed that he had not put any books on the first seat, so he put his 6 yellow books on every fifth seat, starting with the first desk. How many desks have all 3 books? How many have none?

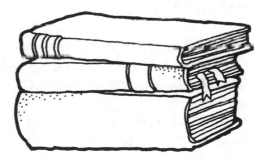

© Prufrock Press Inc • *No Problem!*

## Problem 102

What a sale! Harryberry Shampoo sells in case lots of 6 per case, and So-Clean Soap sells in case lots of 8 bars per case. Ima Spender loves a bargain and she wants to buy a total of 120 bottles and bars. What are the different possible combinations of cases of shampoo and soap that will give her a total of 120 items?

## Problem 103

Matt Ticulous stores his toys in seven brightly colored boxes that are stacked in his closet like the diagram to the right. Using the clues, find the color of each box and place the toys (Lincoln logs, dolls, beads and blocks, paints, puzzles, Construx, and trucks) in the correct box.

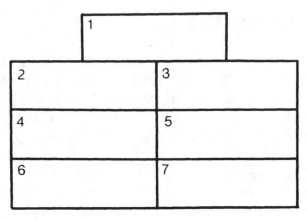

### Clues

1.  Construx is at the top of the pile.
2.  The purple box, is immediately above the trucks on the left side of the pile.
3.  The black box of puzzles is on the left side of the closet, and the pink box is on the right and one level higher than the puzzles.
4.  The gray box is immediately below the beads and blocks.
5.  Box 3 is red.
6.  The bottom right of the closet holds the paints, and the other bottom box is black and does not hold the dolls.
7.  The green box, which has a number less than 6, is to the immediate left of the beads and blocks.
8.  The box with beads and blocks has a number four larger than the blue box.
9.  The pink box is directly below the Lincoln Logs.

## Problem 104

Sue Premacy was running for president of the student council. She worked all evening with her best friend, Jean Jacket, making posters to distribute. Sue gave one-half of the posters to Jean to distribute. She took two-thirds of what was left and left the other 7 for the campaign rally. How many posters did the girls make altogether?

## Problem 105

Benny Fit was in charge of ticket sales for the fund raiser for his school. He sold 120 tickets. The seats in the back of the auditorium only cost $5.00 per ticket, while the better seats went for $8.00 each. He collected $825.00. How many of each kind of ticket did he sell?

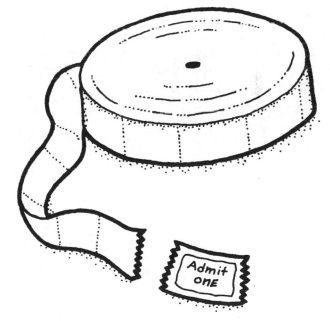

© Prufrock Press Inc • No Problem!

## Problem 106

The library was open and four friends (Sharon, Laren, Darren, and Karen) met at the check-out desk at the same time. They were checking out four books, *Superfudge*, *Cinderella*, *Benji*, and *Where the Wild Things Are*. The librarian mixed up their books. Can you use the clues to figure out which student wanted which book?

### Clues
1. Karen loves Judy Blume books.
2. Laren doesn't like fairy tales.
3. Sharon doesn't like to read about animals or monsters.
4. Darren likes books with short titles for his book reports.

## Problem 107

Little Peg Board is playing quietly with her beads. Peg has 296 beads altogether, and she has 32 more round beads than square beads. How many of each kind of bead does she have?

## Problem 108

Jack Itup, a tire salesman, had three dozen new tires to sell. He wanted a pyramid of tires with one tire at the top and one additional tire in each row. How many of his 36 tires should be put on the bottom row?

## Problem 109

Miles Toogo had directions for getting from his house to Mark T. Map's house across town. He had to take a round-about route to avoid railroad tracks and an industrial park. First he went 2 blocks south and then 2 blocks east. Then he went 4 blocks south, followed by 3 blocks west to get around the industrial park. Then he went 1 block southwest right through the park to Mark's house on the corner. Put an X on Mark's house on your map.

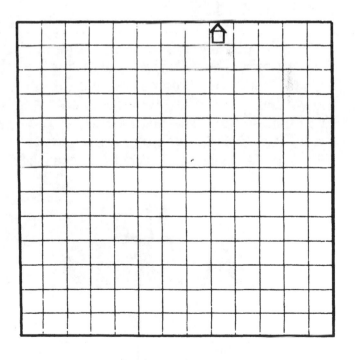

77

## Problem 110

Rosa Seats sells stools and other furniture to restaurants. Some of her stools have 4 legs and others are balanced on only 3 legs. She sold 15 stools this week with a total of 54 legs. How many 3-legged stools and how many 4-legged stools did she sell?

## Problem 111

Four friends always take the same seats in their boat, The *Gill Spill*. All of the friends, Jill, Will, Bill and Lil, like to ride the waves. There are two front seats and two back seats. The steering wheel is on the left side. Bill drives and Jill is next to Will, who is behind Lil. Where do they sit?

© Prufrock Press Inc • *No Problem!*

## Problem 112

Cari Bean was on her way to the islands in her yacht. Because of the waves and the currents, she was making irregular progress. The first day she traveled 100 miles. The second day she traversed 120 miles, and the third day only 90 miles. On the fourth day she made 110 miles, and on the fifth, 80 miles. If this trend continues, how many miles will she have traveled in ten days?

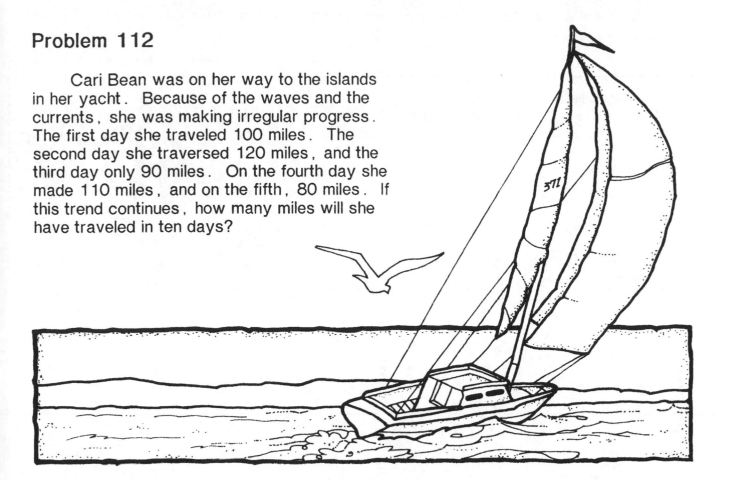

## Problem 113

The Learn to Earn School is going on a field trip to the See-um Museum. The See-um Museum requires that there be at least 1 teacher for every 20 students and 1 chaperon for every 4 students. In addition, the bus company has a bus and driver for every 78 people. There are 316 people who will be going on the trip. How many students, teachers, chaperons, and bus drivers are there?

79

© Prufrock Press Inc • *No Problem!*

## Problem 114

Mac A. Roni purchased three items for lunch from those listed on the menu. He gave the clerk $3.00 and received 10¢ change. What did Mac purchase for lunch?

| Menu | |
|---|---|
| Battered Burger | $1.95 |
| Freaky Fries | $0.65 |
| Crazy Coke | $0.35 |
| Murderous Milk | $0.40 |
| Crunchy Candy | $0.50 |
| Pasted Potatoes | $0.60 |

## Problem 115

Penny Loafer sells shoes at the Feet First Shoe Store and recently set up a prominent display to help sell shoes. One third of the shoes in the front window are high-tops. One third of the shoes in the display are boat shoes. One sixth of the shoes are flats, and eight shoes are sandals. How many shoes are on display in the window?

# Problem 116

There were four cards left out of the deck of cards. There was one card of each suit (spades, hearts, diamonds, and clubs). The card values included an ace, a seven, a ten, and a king. Determine the four cards using these clues:

## Clues
1. The seven and the ace were black cards.
2. The heart had a face on it.
3. The club had a higher value than the other cards.

---

# Problem 117

Three friends, Benny, Denny, and Kenny, have last names of Mills, Sills, and Hills. Each boy owns a dog. The dogs' names are Duke, Rover, and Max, and the dogs are a poodle, a collie, and a spaniel. Using the following clues, determine each boy's full name and the name and type of dog each has.

## Clues
1. Duke is the spaniel.
2. Mills is the last name of Rover's owner.
3. Benny owns the poodle who is not called Max.
4. Kenny's name is not Hills.
5. Denny's dog is not the collie.

© Prufrock Press Inc • *No Problem!*

## Problem 118

Lil E. White just received a delivery of fresh flowers for her party. Before arranging the flowers, she divides them by variety. One fourth (1/4) of the flowers are a dozen long-stemmed roses. Another fourth (1/4) of the flowers are carnations. One eighth (1/8) of the flowers are mums, two eighths (2/8) of the flowers are daisies, two are lilies, and the rest were gardenias. How many of each variety did she receive and how many flowers were there altogether?

## Problem 119

Mrs. Ippi is enrolling her daughter Tippy in school for the first time. There are four different kindergarten teachers, three different 1st grade teachers, and only one second grade teacher at the Prim and Proper Primary School. If all of the teachers remain the same for the next three years, how many different combinations of teachers are possible for Tippy in the next three years?

## Problem 120

Four friends, Dak, Jack, Mack and Zack, got hungry for a snack. At Zack's house, Mrs. Tack offered them raisins, cheese, bananas, and cookies. Each of the boys ate only one of these items, and no boy ate the same thing as any other boy. Dak and Zack don't like fruit, Jack's mom won't let him eat cookies or fresh fruit because of his allergies, and Zack loves cheese. Who ate what?

## Problem 121

Paige Terner checked out a large stack of books for her family. She kept 1/3 of the books for herself. She gave 1/2 of the remaining books to her 5 children. Each child got one book. How many were left for her husband?

83

## Problem 122

Bing O. Player has 3 numbers left to go in the B row for a total blackout and the big Bingo prize of $500.00. Remembering that the B row contains numbers between 1 and 15, figure out what three numbers he has left to be called.

### Clues
1. None of the numbers are even.
2. None of the numbers are a multiple of 5.
3. The sum of the numbers is 31.

## Problem 123

Art Folley is trying to make a paper stained glass window design using 16 squares of colored paper. He has four squares each of four different colors (purple, green, red, and blue). He wants to have one square of each color in any horizontal or vertical row. Show how he can complete the design.

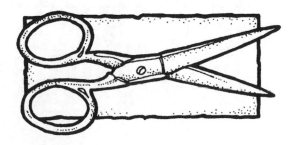

## Problem 124

Kitty Katz works at the Bow and Meow Pet Store. She is in charge of cleaning the dog cages, fish tanks, and bird cages. Altogether she cleans 25 of the pets' homes. Kitty's pets have a total of 46 legs, and 18 of the pets cannot fly. How many are dogs? How many are birds? How many are fish?

## Problem 125

Jill and her older brother Jack play number games to pass the time. One evening they compared their ages. Jack said that in three years he would be twice Jill's age. How old are Jack and Jill now if in three years their combined ages will be 24?

© Prufrock Press Inc · *No Problem!*

## Problem 126

Fay Ling is not going to pass her second semester math class unless she can supply the missing addends and sums in the following grid. Please help her by filling in the missing information.

| + | | | | |
|---|---|---|---|---|
| | 38 | | | 55 |
| 18 | | | 35 | |
| | | 78 | | 66 |
| | 14 | | 19 | |

---

## Problem 127

Della Ware has 50 one-dollar bills that she is supposed to share equally with Mary Land and Vera Mont. The three are sitting in a straight line with Della in the middle and Mary to the right. Della hands the money out by starting with Vera on her left and proceeding: *left, middle, right, middle, left, middle*, etc. Will each of the girls get the same amount? If not, tell how many dollars each of the three girls will receive.

## Problem 128

In the Universe of Cube, all of the major planets are arranged at the vertices of the space routes, which are much like the sides of a cube. If a resident of Cube wishes to travel from Planet A to Planet D using only three routes, how many different travel options are possible?

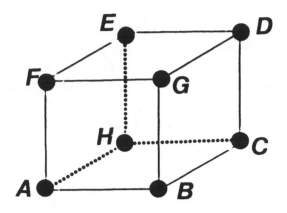

## Problem 129

Kay M. Over wants to see how many different ways there are for dealing four different cards. She has chosen the ace of hearts, the ace of spades, the ace of clubs, and the ace of diamonds. If she always starts or ends with the ace of hearts, how many different combinations are possible?

© Prufrock Press Inc • No Problem!

## Problem 130

Pepe Ronee wants to divide his pizza so that seven people each get a piece of pepperoni. He has been told that he can do this with only three cuts. Show Pepe how to cut the pizza. It's okay if the pieces aren't all the same size, but you cannot slice through a piece of pepperoni.

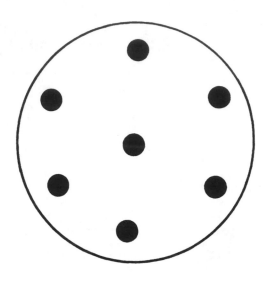

## Problem 131

Reg E. Ment can't remember where to insert the arithmetic symbols between the 6's in each line to make the eight different equations true. In these problems the arithmetic operations should be performed in order from left to right. Insert the symbols to make each number sentence true.

| | | | | |
|---|---|---|---|---|
| 5 = | 6 | 6 | 6 | 6 |
| 8 = | 6 | 6 | 6 | 6 |
| 13 = | 6 | 6 | 6 | 6 |
| 42 = | 6 | 6 | 6 | 6 |
| 48 = | 6 | 6 | 6 | 6 |
| 66 = | 6 | 6 | 6 | 6 |
| 108 = | 6 | 6 | 6 | 6 |
| 180 = | 6 | 6 | 6 | 6 |

## Problem 132

Dolly's age is 5 years less than twice Molly's age. The sum of their ages is 40. How old are Dolly and Molly?

## Problem 133

Hugh Manatee is trying to remember the length and width of the outdoor playing field. He remembers that the perimeter of the rectangular field is 420 yards and that the width is 3/4 of the length. What is the length and the width of the field?

© Prufrock Press Inc • No Problem!

## Problem 134

Anita Vacation needs your help in crossing out 12 of the 36 numbers below so that each row and column is left with exactly four numbers with a sum of 10.

| 2 | 1 | 2 | 2 | 5 | 4 |
|---|---|---|---|---|---|
| 5 | 1 | 1 | 6 | 2 | 3 |
| 3 | 3 | 5 | 1 | 3 | 1 |
| 1 | 7 | 6 | 1 | 1 | 2 |
| 2 | 5 | 1 | 4 | 1 | 3 |
| 4 | 1 | 2 | 4 | 2 | 3 |

## Problem 135

Roland Spin loves to play games with his friend, Harry Bangs. He had planned on playing 10 games with Harry every week, but Harry ends up cancelling 4 of the games during each odd (1st, 3rd, 5th, etc.) week. Roland had planned on playing 100 games in just 10 weeks, but with all of the cancelled games, how many weeks will it take him and Harry to play 100 games?

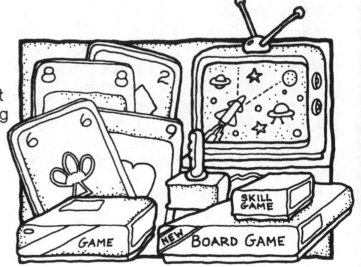

# Student Recording Sheet

Problem Number_____          Name_____

---

Circle the strategy/strategies that you used to solve the problem.

Make an Organized List                    Act Out or Use Objects
Simplify the Problem/Work Backwards       Use or Make a Table
Look for a Pattern                        Use Logic
Make a Diagram or Drawing                 Check and Guess

---

Use this space to show your work.




What is the solution?




Does your answer fit the problem?  Is there a way to check your work?

          © Prufrock Press Inc • *No Problem!*

# Answers

## Problem 49
Billy can number 90 balls.

## Problem 50
There are 27 possible combinations as follows:
111, 114, 117, 141, 144, 147, 171, 174, 177,
411, 414, 417, 441, 444, 447, 471, 474, 477,
711, 714, 717, 741, 744, 747, 771, 774, 777

## Problem 51
From left to right, the fabrics are:
red, white, black print, orange, plaid, yellow

## Problem 52
There are 12 combinations. They are:
Corvette silver convertible
Corvette green convertible
Jaguar silver convertible
Jaguar green convertible
Porsche silver convertible
Porsche green convertible
Corvette silver sun-roof
Corvette green sun-roof
Jaguar silver sun-roof
Jaguar green sun-roof
Porsche silver sun-roof
Porsche green sun-roof

## Problem 53
There are 14 tents, 7 north of their tent and 6 tents to the south.

## Problem 54
The princess is rescued on the 7th day

| Day | 1 | 2 | 3 | 4 | 5 | 6 | 7 |
|-----|---|---|---|---|---|---|---|
| Level | 1 | 3 | 7 | 13 | 21 | 31 | 42 |

## Problem 55
18 combinations

## Problem 56
24 ribbons and 41 barrettes

## Problem 57
In the list below, the first column is quarters, the second is dimes, the third is nickels, the fourth is pennies, and the last column is the total number of coins used.
1 1 1 6 = 9 coins
1 1 2 1 = 5 coins
1 2 0 1 = 4 coins
1 0 4 1 = 6 coins
1 0 3 6 = 10 coins

## Problem 58
Max's sandwich will have 18 pieces of cold cuts when Pat's sandwich has 9 pieces of cold cuts.

## Problem 59
27 different ways

## Problem 60

| | Al | Paul |
|-------|----|------|
| Day 1 | 3 | 9 |
| Day 2 | 6 | 18 |
| Day 3 | 12 | 27 |
| Day 4 | 24 | 36 |
| Day 5 | 48 | 45 |
| Day 6 | 96 | 64 |
| Day 7 | Al wins | 73 |

## Problem 61
Aries - 4
Scorpio - 17
Leo -10
Centaurus - 14

## Problem 62

| blue | green | silver |
|------|-------|--------|
| yellow | white | red |

## Problem 63
7 chairs and 4 tables

## Problem 64
6 hours a day

## Problem 65
There are 25 possibilities. If the first number is the number of touchdowns, the second number is the number of points after the touchdown, the third number is the number of field goals, and the last is the number of safeties, the possibilities are:

| | | |
|------|------|-------|
| 4000 | 2114 | 1026 |
| 3310 | 2040 | 1009 |
| 3202 | 2023 | 0080 |
| 3111 | 2006 | 0063 |
| 3020 | 1151 | 0046 |
| 3003 | 1134 | 0029 |
| 2222 | 1117 | 000 12 |
| 2205 | 1060 | |
| 2131 | 1043 | |

## Problem 66
180 possibilities

## Problem 67
13 days

## Problem 68
120 swimmers in the deep end and 60 swimmers in the shallow end

## Problem 69
The number is 69.

## Problem 70
The glasses from left to right belong to:
A–Jan  B–Dan  C–Nan  D–Stan  E–Van  F–Fran

## Problem 71

| △ | ◆ | ○ | ★ | △ | ◆ |
|---|---|---|---|---|---|
| ◆ | ○ | ★ | △ | ◆ | ○ |
| ○ | ★ | △ | ◆ | ○ | ★ |
| ★ | △ | ◆ | ○ | ★ | △ |
| △ | ◆ | ○ | ★ | △ | ◆ |

## Problem 72
From left to right, the answers are:
A-Carleen  B-Darlene  C-Marleen  D-Sharlene

## Problem 73
48 invitations

## Problem 74
62 scallop and 37 conch shells

## Problem 75
4,095 pennies

## Problem 76
3 combinations – They are:
9,7, and 5
9,8, and 4
8,7, and 6

## Problem 77
The numbers are 1441 and 3223

## Problem 78
232 exercises (30 + 25 + 27 + 22 + 24 + 30 + 25 + 27 + 22)

## Problem 79
76 monsters
The pattern is to increase 2 monsters one day and then increase 7 monsters the next day.

## Problem 80
36 ways

## Problem 81
Children's tickets – $15.00 each
Adult tickets – $30.00 each

## Problem 82

Polly (c)
Patty (b)
Penny (a)

Peppy (d)
Perry (e)
Pinky (f)
Percy (g)

## Problem 83
14 correct responses

## Problem 84
Chip and Van each ate 2 cookies each and Ginger ate 3 cookies.

## Problem 85
8 pewter pieces and 3 lead pieces

## Problem 86
13 or 14 bags, depending on the number of Sundays in the year.

## Problem 87
Starting at the bottom circle and moving clockwise, the answers are:
6/12  1/12  5/12  3/12  4/12  2/12

## Problem 88
They will see each other again in 5 weeks.

## Problem 89
16 different combinations are possible

## Problem 90
lemon drops
gumballs
root beer barrels

licorice sticks
rock candy
orange slices

## Problem 91
The number is 36.

## Problem 92
Pat had 160 signatures and Cam had 80 signatures

## Problem 93
224 squares

## Problem 94
Nan – Siamese
Jan – tabby
Dan – German shephord
Fran – beagle

## Problem 95
13 applications for dishwasher
26 applications for secretary
39 applications for gardener

## Problem 96
Sir Quacky – 21 inches
Sir Lancealittle – 18 inches
Sir Rustedout – 12 inches

## Problem 97
18 combinations

## Problem 98
The boys are in two adjacent trees. Roger is in the 8th tree of the 6th row, and Will is in the 8th tree of the 5th row.

## Problem 99
Ten (10) different combinations are possible.

## Problem 100
Holly
Polly
Golly

Rolly
Molly
Olly
Mrs. Ellie Gator

## Problem 101
Only one (1) desk has all three books and eight (8) desks have none.

## Problem 102
There are four possiblities: 8 cases of Harryberry Shampoo, 9 cases of So–Clean Soap
4 shampoo and 12 soap
8 shampoo and 9 soap
12 shampoo and 6 soap
16 shampoo and 3 soap

## Problem 103
Box 1 – blue, Construx
Box 2 – purple, dolls
Box 3 – red, Lincoln Logs
Box 4 – green, trucks
Box 5 – pink, beads and blocks
Box 6 – black, puzzles
Box 7 – gray, paints

## Problem 104
42 posters

## Problem 105
He sold 75 of the $8.00 tickets and 45 of the $5.00 tickets.

## Problem 106
Karen – *Superfudge*
Sharon – *Cinderella*
Darren – *Benji*
Laren – *Where the Wild Things Are*

## Problem 107
164 round beads and 132 square beads

## Problem 108
8 tires on the bottom row

## Problem 109
Mark's house is 7 spaces south and 2 to the west of the starting point.

## Problem 110
Six 3–legged stools and nine 4–legged stools

## Problem 111
Bill        Lil
Jill        Will

## Problem 112
900 miles altogether

## Problem 113
There were 12 teachers, 240 students, 60 chaperons, and 4 bus drivers.

## Problem 114
Mac bought one battered burger, one pasted potato, and one crazy coke.

## Problem 115
48 shoes are on display – 16 hightops, 16 boat shoes, 8 flats, 8 sandles.

## Problem 116
The seven is a spade
The king is a heart
The ten is a diamond
The ace is a club

## Problem 117
Benny Mills owns a poodle named Rover
Denny Hills owns a spaniel named Duke
Kenny Sills owns a collie named Max

## Problem 118
Lil received 48 flowers altogether:
12 roses          6 mums
12 carnations     2 lilies
12 daisies        4 gardenias

## Problem 119
12 combinations of teachers

## Problem 120
Dak – cookie
Jack – raisins
Mack – banana
Zack – cheese

## Problem 121
Paige checked out a total of 15 books; 5 for herself, five for her children, and 5 books left for her husband.

## Problem 122
Bing needs the numbers: 7, 11 and 13

## Problem 123
There are several possible answers.

## Problem 124
Kitty takes care of 8 dogs, 7 birds, and 10 fish.

## Problem 125
Jack is 13 and Jill is 5.

## Problem 126

| +  | 12 | 41 | 17 | 29 |
|----|----|----|----|----|
| 26 | 38 | 67 | 43 | 55 |
| 18 | 30 | 59 | 35 | 47 |
| 37 | 49 | 78 | 54 | 66 |
| 2  | 14 | 43 | 19 | 31 |

## Problem 127
The money will not be divided equally.
Mary will receive $12.00.
Della will receive $25.00.
Vera will receive $13.00.

## Problem 128
There are 6 ways to get from A to D.

## Problem 129
12 different combinations (6 with the ace of hearts dealt first and 6 with the ace of hearts dealt last)

**Problem 130**

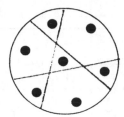

**Problem 131**
 5 = {(6 x 6) − 6} ÷ 6
 8 = {(6 + 6) ÷ 6} + 6
13 = (6 ÷ 6) + 6 + 6
42 = {(6 ÷ 6) + 6} x 6
48 = (6 x 6) + 6 + 6
66 = {(6 + 6) x 6} − 6
108 = (6 + 6 + 6) x 6
180 = {(6 x 6) − 6} x 6

**Problem 132**
Dolly is 25 and Molly is 15.

**Problem 133**
The length is 120 yards and the width is 90 yards.

**Problem 134**
1st row − cross out the last 2 and 4
2nd row − cross out the 6 and the 2
3rd row − cross out the first two 3's
4th row − cross out the 6 and the 2
5th row − cross out the 5 and the first 1
6th row − cross out the first 4 and the last 2

**Problem 135**
They will complete 100 games during the 13th week.

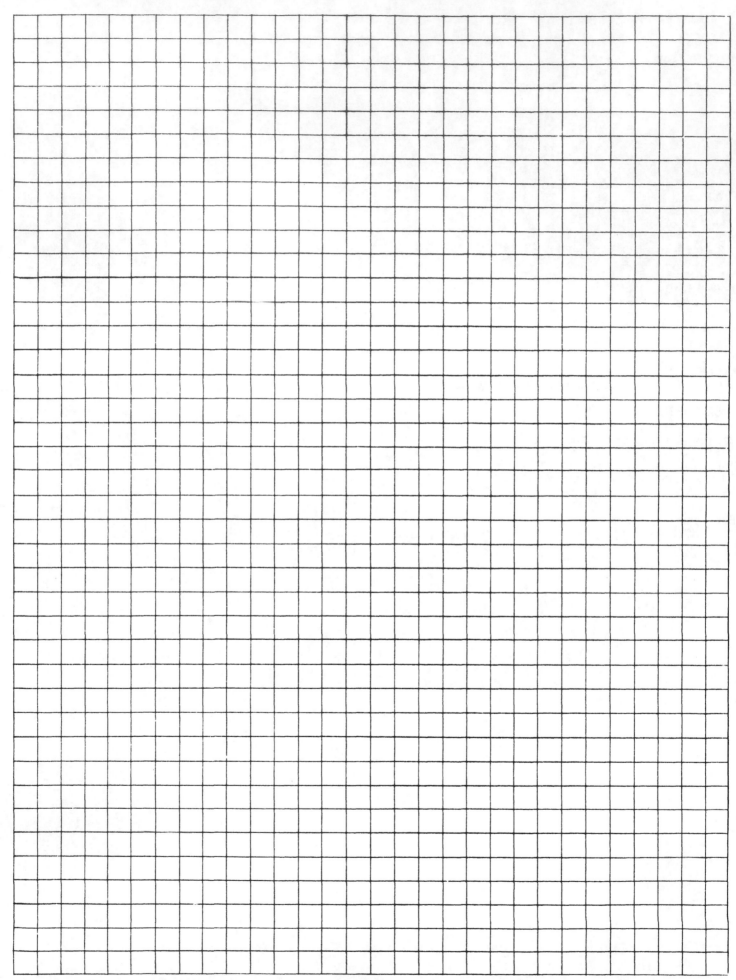

# Common Core State Standards Alignment Sheet
## No Problem!

| Week | Common Core State Standards in Math |
|---|---|
| Week 1: Guess and Check | 4.OA.A Use the four operations with whole numbers to solve problems.<br>4.MD.A Solve problems involving measurement and conversion of measurements. |
| Week 2: Use or Make a Table | 4.OA.A Use the four operations with whole numbers to solve problems.<br>4.OA.B Gain familiarity with factors and multiples.<br>6.RP.A Understand ratio concepts and use ratio reasoning to solve problems. |
| Week 3: Make an Organized List | 4.OA.A Use the four operations with whole numbers to solve problems.<br>4.NBT.A Generalize place value understanding for multi-digit whole numbers.<br>4.MD.A Solve problems involving measurement and conversion of measurements. |
| Week 4: Look for a Pattern | 4.OA.C Generate and analyze patterns.<br>5.OA.B Analyze patterns and relationships. |
| Week 5: Act Out/ Use Manipulatives | None applicable. |
| Week 6: Use Logic | None applicable. |
| Week 7: Simplify or Work Backwards | 4.NF.B Build fractions from unit fractions.<br>4.MD.A Solve problems involving measurement and conversion of measurements.<br>5.NF.B Apply and extend previous understandings of multiplication and division.<br>5.MD.A Convert like measurement units within a given measurement system.<br>6.RP.A Understand ratio concepts and use ratio reasoning to solve problems. |
| Week 8: Make a Diagram or Drawing | 4.MD.A Solve problems involving measurement and conversion of measurements.<br>6.RP.A Understand ratio concepts and use ratio reasoning to solve problems.<br>6.NS.C Apply and extend previous understandings of numbers to the system of rational numbers. |
| Year-Long Program | 4.OA.A Use the four operations with whole numbers to solve problems.<br>4.OA.C Generate and analyze patterns.<br>4.NBT.A Generalize place value understanding for multi-digit whole numbers.<br>4.NF.B Build fractions from unit fractions.<br>4.MD.A Solve problems involving measurement and conversion of measurements.<br>5.NF.B Apply and extend previous understandings of multiplication and division.<br>6.RP.A Understand ratio concepts and use ratio reasoning to solve problems.<br>6.EE.A Apply and extend previous understandings of arithmetic to algebraic expressions.<br>7.RP.A Analyze proportional relationships and use them to solve real-world and mathematical problems.<br>7.SP.C Investigate chance processes and develop, use, and evaluate probability models. |

**Key:** OA = Operations & Algebraic Thinking; NBT = Number & Operations in Base Ten; NF = Number & Operations--Fractions; MD = Measurement & Data; RP = Ratios & Proportional Relationships; NS = The Number System; EE = Expressions & Equations; SP = Statistics & Probability

Printed in the United States
by Baker & Taylor Publisher Services